COMMON SENSE IN CHESS

COMMON SENSE
IN CHESS

BY

Emanuel Lasker

REVISED BY
Fred Reinfeld

Frontispiece by Maximilian Mopp

DAVID McKAY COMPANY, INC.
NEW YORK

Preface

THE FOLLOWING is an abstract of Twelve Lectures given before an audience of London chess players during the spring of 1895. It may be regarded as an attempt to deal with all parts of a game of chess by the aid of general principles. The principles laid down are deduced from considerations concerning the nature of Chess as a fight between two brains, and their conception is based on simple facts. Their practical working has been illustrated by positions adapted to the purpose, and likely to occur over the board.

It has been my aim to reduce the different rules in number as much as was compatible with clearness. They all, it will be found, have a remote likeness, and it would therefore not have been very difficult to reduce their number still more. Indeed, they may ultimately be united in one single leading principle, which is the germ of the theory not only of Chess, but of any kind of fight. This principle is sufficiently indicated here, but it is so general in its conception, and the difficulty of expressing the whole compass of its meaning in definite terms so enormous, that I have not ventured to formulate it. In a future work, for which the present one shall pave the way, I hope to be able to illustrate the significance of that principle, and its capacity for showing facts in their right relation to one another. For that work I have also deferred the discussion of some points which require very nice differentiation, such as all questions relating to the maneuvering of the King and the exchange of men.

The games and positions given in this book are comparatively few, but they have been selected with care. I therefore would advise the student not to attempt to *read* the matter only, but to *study* it and sink some work into it. The rules deduced are, I believe, very plausible. This need not deceive the student, who will see their significance in a clearer light if he tries to be reasonably skeptical and exacting in the matter of proofs.

As regards the analytical notes about games or openings, I have tried to be short and to the point. Analytical detail is therefore not abundant, but, I think, reliable. The method of enumerating *all* the variations thought possible, or probable, has been laid aside, and in its place an analysis has been given, which makes use of both the consideration of the leading variations *and* general principles. The diction and style of the work are those of a lecturer. Feeling that I have not been able to make them as perfect as I should have desired, I must ask for the lenient judgment of the reader.

I take this opportunity for expressing my hearty thanks to Professor Villin Marmery for his kind assistance in looking over the proofs.

EMANUEL LASKER

Introduction

OF THE thousands of books that have been written on chess, the vast majority have had a passing vogue, while a relatively small number are recognized as classics. They continue to be read long after they were published, long after their authors have died. "Common Sense In Chess" is such a book. It has continued to be read because its method of presentation was based on an original idea: Lasker was interested in setting forth valuable *principles*, rather than the myriad petty details which only obfuscate the material and confuse the reader.

The object of this revision has therefore been to preserve all that was useful in the first edition; to prune out palpable errors; to modernize the work in the spirit in which it was originally written. Every change has accordingly been weighed carefully. The most radical departure has naturally been in the realm of the openings, in which there have been so many advances that the original material had lost much of its value for the reader. The revised edition is now presented to a new generation in the conviction that "Common Sense In Chess" will prove more helpful than ever to players of all degrees of skill.

FRED REINFELD

New York,
June 4, 1945

Contents

1. General Principles of Opening Play

I T I S C U S T O M A R Y to begin with definitions, but I
am sure that all of you are so well acquainted with the
essential parts of the history, the rules and the characteristics of Chess, that you will allow me to jump at once
in medias res. Chess has been represented, or shall I say
misrepresented, as a game—that is, a thing which could
not well serve a serious purpose, solely created for the
enjoyment of an empty hour. If it were a game only,
Chess would never have survived the serious trials to
which it has, during the long time of its existence, been
often subjected. By some ardent enthusiasts Chess has
been elevated into a science or an art. It is neither; but its
principal characteristic seems to be—what human nature
mostly delights in—a fight. Not a fight, indeed, such as
would tickle the nerves of coarser natures, where blood
flows and the blows delivered leave their visible traces on
the bodies of the combatants, but a fight in which the
scientific, the artistic, the purely intellectual element
holds undivided sway. From this standpoint, a game of
Chess becomes a harmonious whole, the outlines of which
I will endeavor to describe to you in this course of lectures.

The requisites in Chess are a board of sixty-four
squares, and two bodies of men. We have, therefore, one
great advantage over the general who is to lead an army
into the field—we know where to find the enemy, and the
strength at his disposal. We have the gratifying knowledge that as far as material strength is concerned we shall

be equal to our opponents. Nevertheless, our first step will be exactly analogous to that of a commander of an army. First of all we shall mobilize our troops, make them ready for action, try to seize the important lines and points which are yet wholly unoccupied. This proceeding will take, as a rule, no more than six moves, as we shall see later on. If we should neglect to do so, our opponent would avail himself of the opportunity thus given him, would quickly assail some vital point, and ere we could rally, the battle would be finished.

Let me, in illustration of my assertions, go over some well known little games, in which mistakes and the punishment thereof are clearly traceable.

WHITE	BLACK
1. P - K4	P - K4
2. Kt - KB3	P - Q3
3. B - B4	P - KR3 ?

So far, with the exception of the last move, Black has played quite well. He has opened lines for his two Bishops and the Queen, and now should bring out his QKt to B3. Instead of that, afraid of some premature attack, he quite unnecessarily makes a move that does not give additional force to any of his pieces.

4. Kt - B3	B - Kt5 ?

A mistake. The Knights should be first developed, then the Bishops.

5. Kt x P !!	B x Q ?
6. B x P ch	K - K2
7. Kt - Q5 mate	

Another tune to the same theme:

WHITE	BLACK
1. P - K4	P - K4
2. Kt - KB3	Kt - KB3
3. Kt x P	Kt - B3

Black evidently believes in the principle of quick development, and even neglects to win back his Pawn, in order to gain time.

4. Kt x Kt	QP x Kt
5. P - Q3	B - QB4
6. B - Kt5 ?	

A mistake; he ought to guard against the threatened Kt - Kt5 with B - K2. Now he is overtaken by a catastrophe.

6. . . .	Kt x P !!
7. B x Q	B x P ch
8. K - K2	B - Kt5 mate

Another variation:

WHITE	BLACK
1. P - K4	P - K4
2. P - KB4	P x P

White, in order to aid his development, sacrifices a Pawn. Whether with good reason or not, we shall not argue for the present.

3. B - B4	Q - R5 ch
4. K - B1	P - Q4

An excellent move. Black also sacrifices a Pawn, to invest it, so to say, in facilities for bringing out his pieces.

5. B x P	P - KKt4
6. Kt - KB3	Q - R4
7. P - KR4	

A good move, which gives our Rook something to do. The attack on Black's Pawn, however, is only an apparent one for the moment, because both the Kt and KRP are pinned.

| 7. . . . | P - KR3 ? |

He ought to develop a piece, for instance, B - Kt2. This omission will cost him the game.

B L A ᐧ C K

W H I T E

| 8. B x P ch ! | Q x B |

Not K x B ?? on account of (9) Kt - K5 ch.

9. Kt - K5	Q - Kt2
10. Q - R5 ch	K - K2
11. Kt - Kt6 ch	K - Q1
12. Kt x R	Q x Kt
13. P x P	

And now we have two Pawns and an excellently placed Rook for two pieces, while Black's pieces are all still at home, and his King in an unsafe position. Between fairly even players the issue of the game is therefore decided in favor of White.

Let me go over some moves which frequently occur in games of a close character.

FRENCH DEFENSE
(*Nurnberg, 1883*)

WHITE	BLACK
Fritz	*Mason*
1. P - K4	P - K3
2. P - Q4	P - Q4
3. Kt - QB3	Kt - KB3
4. B - Kt5	B - K2

An equally solid and safe continuation is (4) . . . P x P, (5) Kt x P, B - K2 etc.

5. B x Kt	B x B
6. Kt - KB3	

P - K5 followed by Q - Kt4 yields stronger attacking chances.

6. . . .	Castles
7. B - Q3	P - QKt3

The right move was (7) . . . P - B4! If then (8) P - K5, B - K2; (9) P x P, Kt - Q2 ! (10) P - KR4, P - B4 ! (11) P x P e.p., B x P and Black has nothing to fear. Thus if (12) B x P ch ? K x B; (13) Kt - Kt5 ch, K - Kt1; (14)

Q - R5, B x Kt ch; (15) P x B, Kt - B3 and White is a piece down and his attack is spent.

Here we have a good example of the way in which efficient and carefully considered development can repulse a premature attack.

8. P - K5   B - K2
9. P - KR4

White consistently takes aim against Black's K side. Black's Q side pieces have so little bearing upon the actual scene of battle that his game is already greatly compromised.

9. . . .   B - Kt2 ?

The only comparatively safe move would have been B - R3 !

Black: MASON

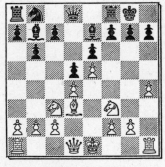

White: FRITZ

10. B x P ch !   K·x B
11. Kt - Kt5 ch   K ◄Kt3

If instead K - Kt1; (12) Q - R5, B x Kt; (13) P x B, P - B3; (14) P - Kt6, and mate cannot be avoided.

12. Kt - K2 !	B x Kt
13. P x B	P - KB4

If Q x P; (14) Kt - B4 ch !, K - B4; (15) Q - Q3 ch, K - Kt5; (16) Q - R3 ch, K x Kt; (17) Q B3 mate.

14. KtP x P e.p.	K - B2
15. Kt - B4	R - R1

To protect himself against White playing R - KR7. But his defense is of no avail, as his cruel foe does not allow him a moment's repose.

16. Q - Kt4 !!	R x R ch
17. K - Q2	P x P

What shall he do? If R - R2; (18) Q x KP ch, K - B1; (19) Kt - Kt6 mate.

18. Q - Kt6 ch	K - K2
19. Q - Kt7 ch	K - K1
20. Q - Kt8 ch	K - K2
21. Q x P ch	K - B1

First White drives the Black K into the most dangerous spot, and then comes the finishing stroke—

22. R x R	K - Kt2
23. R - R7 ch !	K x R
24. Q - B7 ch	K - R1
25. Kt - Kt6 mate.	

If we again critically glance over the few variations that we have gone through, we must be struck by one fact, namely, that *the losing side had the greater part of his army in positions where they had no bearing whatever upon the questions at issue. They might have been just as well anywhere else but on the board.* I have formulated the rules for the development of the pieces according to my own experience over the board, and, I think, also in accordance with established facts, in the following manner:—

    I. Do not move any Pawns in the opening of a game but the K and the Q Pawns.

   II. Do not move any piece twice in the opening, but put it at once upon the right square.

       (In my practice I have usually found it strongest to post the Kts at B3, where they have a magnificent sway, and the KB somewhere on his original diagonal, if not exposed to exchange, at QB4.)

  III. Bring your Kts out before developing the Bishops, especially the QB.

  IV. Do not pin the adverse KKt (by B - KKt5) before your opponent has castled.

In regard to Rule I you will sometimes, especially in Q side openings, find it a better plan to advance the QBP two squares before obstructing it by your QKt. This, however, is the only exception, where the violation of the principles just laid down, is unquestionably justified. You will see that, according to this plan, the mobilization takes altogether six moves, consumed in the development of two Pawns, the two Knights, and the two Bishops. You may be obliged to spend some of your time in the beginning of a game for the exchange of a Pawn or a piece, or it may be necessary to make one or two defensive moves. But the real business of development ought to be accomplished in no more than six separate moves devoted to that purpose.

2. *Ruy Lopez* (BERLIN DEFENSE)

W E H A V E given in the previous chapter the theory of
the first part of a game of Chess, and have, to a certain
extent, attempted to prove and to illustrate it. It now remains to put it to practical test. For this purpose I shall
discuss a popular form of opening called the Ruy Lopez,
from the name of the Spanish bishop who invented it.
It consists of the following three moves:—

WHITE	BLACK
1. P - K4	P - K4
2. Kt - KB3	Kt - QB3
3. B - Kt5	

Of course you will at once perceive that the threat,
which White's last move seems to imply, viz., B x Kt, followed by Kt x P, is only an apparent one, as Black will
regain his Pawn easily. We are, therefore, at liberty to
make any developing move we please. The best defense
is (3) . . . P - QR3, making it possible to drive away
White's KB later on. At first sight (3) . . . P - QR3 vio-
lates one of the previously listed rules of development,
but, since it compels White to lose time as well, Black's
development is not adversely affected.

3. . . .	Kt - B3

White's next move may be (4) Kt - B3, or P - Q3, which
would give him a solid and, on the whole, strong game.
But these variations would not present any special difficulty to Black, who could continue, for instance, with
P - Q3 and afterward adopt exactly the tactics recommended in the first chapter. White has, however, other

continuations at his disposal which give him a harassing attack, which Black must exercise great judgment to meet.

4. Castles

What is Black to do next? According to our principles he may play B - K2, and actually this move may be made without any real danger. But this is not the question at issue. The Black KKt attacks the White KP, which White has left unguarded. Is Black to accept the offer? I consider this matter at some length, because it frequently presents itself, for instance, in all gambits.

4. . . .   Kt x P

This move exposes Black to some danger, because he loses valuable time guarding or retreating this Knight.

5. R - K1

Not the best move, but one that most naturally suggests itself.

5. . . .   Kt - Q3

To gain time by the attack on the White Bishop.

6. Kt - B3   Kt x B

BLACK

WHITE

7. Kt x P !

Cunning play. If Black now takes one of the Knights he loses, *e. g.*,

A	7. . . .	KKt x Kt
	8. Kt x Kt ch	B - K2
	9. Kt x B !	Kt x Q
	10. Kt - Kt6 ch	Q - K2
	11. Kt x Q and remains a piece ahead	
B	7. . . .	QKt x Kt
	8. R x Kt ch	B - K2
	9. Kt - Q5 !	Castles
	10. Kt x B ch	K - R1

Now see White's mode of attack, which is rather instructive and of frequent occurrence.

> 11. Q - R5   P - KKt3

(11) . . . P - KR3 was somewhat better.

> 12. Q - R6   P - Q3

White mates in two. Which is the move?

> 13. R - R5 !   P x R
> 14. Q - B6 mate

Return to the position at Black's 7th move.

BLACK

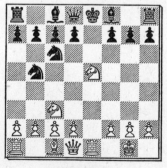

WHITE

7. . . .   B - K2

We thus intercept the dangerous file against our King and develop a piece—two great advantages.

8. Kt - Q5	Castles
9. Kt x Kt	QP x Kt
10. Kt x B ch	K - R1
11. Kt x B	Q x Kt
12. P - Q3	Q - B4
13. B - K3	KR - K1

And Black's game is, if anything, preferable. You see how quickly White's attack has spent itself out. But then he did not make the best of his position at move 5. Let us therefore return to that point.

BLACK

WHITE

5. P - Q4

We develop and attack at the same time, while our Pawn cannot be taken, viz.: (5) . . . P x P; (6) R - K1, P - B4; (7) B x Kt, QP x B; (8) Kt x P, threatening P - KB3, and should win.

5. . . .   B - K2

Kt - Q3 instead leads to an early exchange of Queens. The resulting position is about even, viz.: (5) . . . Kt - Q3; (6) B x Kt, QP x B; (7) P x P, Kt - B4; (8) Q x Q ch,

K x Q; (9) R - Q1 ch, K - K1; (10) Kt - B3, B - K2; (11) P - KR3, P - KR3, etc.

6. Q - K2

The last move is more aggressive than P x P at once, which would allow Black time to do anything he pleases, for instance, to castle at once, or to advance P - Q4. Consider the following variation as an example of what is likely to follow after: (6) P x P, P - Q4; (7) P x P *e.p.*, Kt x QP; (8) B x Kt ch, P x B; (9) Kt - K5, B - Kt2, and Black's pieces are excellently placed.

6. . . .	Kt - Q3
7. B x Kt	KtP x B

not QP x B, which would open the Q file to White's Rook, *e. g.*, (7) . . . QP x B; (8) P x P, Kt - B4; (9) R - Q1, B - Q2.

The Black QB and Q are now so badly placed that White has an opportunity of bringing the game to a virtual finish by energetic attack: (10) P - K6, P x P; (11) Kt - K5, threatening both the Bishop and Q - R5 ch, and should therefore win.

8. P x P	Kt - Kt2

BLACK

WHITE

The position now arrived at is unfavorable for Black for a number of reasons:

1. While White's development can proceed in perfectly normal fashion, Black's prospects are rather forbidding: his Knight must lose two more moves to reach the center; his QB is temporarily stalemated; and quite some time must elapse before this piece will be ready for action.

2. Black's Queen-side Pawns are weak, and this is particularly true of his prospects for the ending, where he will be handicapped by the awkward and rather helpless doubled Pawns.

3. White's advanced KP exercises a formidably cramping effect on White's position, and in some cases the presence of this Pawn will notably facilitate the formation of a strong King-side attack.

Here are some plausible variations:

I

9. Kt - Q4		Castles
10. R - Q1		Q - K1
11. R - K1		

To prevent either . . . P - B3 or . . . P - Q4.

11. . . .		Kt - B4

Not to be recommended, although in frequent use.

12. Kt - QB3		B - R3
13. Q - Kt4		Kt - K3
14. Kt - B5		K - R1
15. Kt - K4		

White has a powerful King-side attack. Black is handicapped by the awkward and ineffectual position of his pieces.

BLACK

WHITE

And Black is quite helpless against the threat R - K3 - KR3 etc.

II

9. Kt - Q4	Castles
10. R - Q1	Q - K1
11. R - K1	Kt - B4
12. Kt - QB3	Kt - K3
13. Kt - B5	P - Q4
14. P x P e.p.	P x P
15. Q - Kt4	P - Kt3
16. B - R6	Kt - Kt2
17. Kt x B ch	Q x Kt
18. Q - Q4	

White wins at least the exchange.

III

9. Kt - Q4	O - O
10. Kt - QB3	B - B4
11. R - Q1	B x Kt

The indicated continuation, if he is to try to get his Knight into play.

12. R x B	P - Q4
13. P x P e.p.	P x P
14. P - QKt4 !	

Very strong. The unfortunate Knight is kept out of play.

14. . . .	Q - B3
15. B - K3	B - B4
16. QR - Q1	

BLACK

WHITE

White has a beautiful game, while Black's position is riddled with Pawn weaknesses and his development leaves much to be desired.

Thus we conclude that the defense 3 . . . Kt - B3 is unsatisfactory for Black.

3. *Ruy Lopez*
(MORPHY AND STEINITZ DEFENSES)

THIS CHAPTER continues the study of the Ruy Lopez, which has enjoyed immense popularity for many years. Its object is to exert pressure on Black's game from the very start—a pressure which can often become exceedingly uncomfortable for the defender.

1. P - K4	P - K4
2. Kt - KB3	Kt - QB3
3. B - Kt5	

As we shall see, this move does not threaten to win the KP, but it threatens to . . . threaten.

3. . . .	P - QR3

It has been pointed out previously that this move does not really lose time, since White must either retreat his KB (which contributes nothing to his development) or exchange, in which case (4) . . . QP x B opens up the diagonal of Black's QB and may thus be considered a developing move.

4. B - R4

Note that (4) B x Kt, QP x B; (5) Kt x P does not win a Pawn; Black can regain it with at least equality by playing (5) . . . Q - Kt4 or (5) . . . Q - Q5.

An interesting possibility here is (4) B x Kt, QP x B; (5) P - Q4, P x P; (6) Q x P, Q x Q; (7) Kt x Q and we reach an endgame in which the respective chances are

balanced fairly evenly: Black has two valuable Bishops
which will be a distinct asset, while White has the better
Pawn position. His four Pawns to three on the King-side
should result in a passed Pawn in due course; the same
cannot be said for Black's Queen-side, because of the fact
that the QBP is doubled.

4. . . .   Kt - B3
5. Castles

BLACK

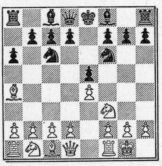

WHITE

There was still no point in trying to win the KP, as
White's KP was attacked as well.

Now we come to a parting of the ways, as Black has
two distinct modes of procedure open to him.

I

5. . . .   B - K2

This is the more solid way of continuing. Black develops his KB and prepares to castle.

6. R - K1

Guarding his KP and therefore really threatening to
win Black's KP by B x Kt followed by Kt x P.

An alternative which has gained considerable favor in
recent years is (6) Q - K2, with the likely continuation
(6) . . . P - QKt4; (7) B - Kt3, P - Q3; (8) P - B3.
White's plan is to proceed with R - Q1 and P - Q4—a very
promising idea.

6. . . .	P - QKt4
7. B - Kt3	P - Q3

Black's last two moves have effectually disposed of any
possible danger to his KP.

8. P - B3

This move has the double object of preparing a broad
Pawn center with P - Q4, and also preserving the KB
against (8) . . . Kt - QR4, which would force the exchange of the useful KB.

8. . . .	Kt - QR4

If instead (8) . . . Castles; (9) P - Q4, B - Kt5; (10)
P - Q5, Kt - QR4; (11) B - B2, P - B3; (12) P x P, Kt x BP;
(13) QKt - Q2 and White's position is preferable.

9. B - B2	P - B4

This is really the point of Black's previous move. The
text creates ample maneuvering space for Black's pieces
on the Queenside.

10. P - Q4	Q - B2

Giving the KP needed protection and at the same time
preparing for future action on the QB file.

11. P - KR3

White wishes to avoid any inconvenience resulting
from a future pin by the hostile QB.

11. . . .	Castles
12. QKt - Q2	BP x P
13. P x P	Kt - B3
14. P - Q5	Kt - QKt5

Apparently risky, but it is all according to plan.

15. B - Kt1	P - QR4

White was threatening to win this Knight with P - R3.

16. P - R3	Kt - R3

This is one of the best defensive systems against the Lopez, and the position is about even. Black's QKt is momentarily poorly posted, but will soon find an excellent square at QB4. The prospective struggle for the QB file is likely to lead to an exchange of all the Rooks. Black's most frequent difficulty in this opening, exposure to a lasting King-side attack, is ruled out here.

II
(See the Diagram on Page 18.)

5. . . .	Kt x P

This is more aggressive and also more risky than (5) . . . B - K2.

6. P - Q4

He can recover the Pawn at once with (6) R - K1 or (6) Q - K2, but Black would have an easy game with (6) . . . Kt - B4.

The object of the text is to get Black's KKt into hot water by means of a possible pin on the K file; also, the advance of the QP helps White's development.

6. . . .	P - QKt4

The immediate (6) . . . P - Q4 would be bad because of (7) Kt x P with strong pressure on Black's game.

Likewise, (6) . . . P x P would be much too dangerous in view of (7) R - K1, P - Q4; (8) Kt x P threatening

(9) P - KB3 and (9) Kt x Kt with catastrophic results for
Black. Such "self-pinning" tactics usually court disaster
and are best avoided.

7. B - Kt3	P - Q4
8. P x P	B K3
9. P - B3	

To preserve the KB from exchange; he also creates a
strong point for his pieces at Q4.

BLACK

WHITE

The position now arrived at is intensely interesting because of the sharply outlined clarity with which each side
can pursue its goals:

White hopes for a King-side attack, based on the
powerful position of his KP, supported by the advance
P - KB4 - 5; the elimination of Black's well placed Knight
on K5; and in some cases, pressure on Black's QB4, which
is a hole (that is, unprotected by Pawns).

Black believes that he has ample resources to carry a
King-side attack, and in some cases he may even snatch
the initiative himself by means of . . . P - KB3 or . . .
P - KB4; he will try to maintain his KKt at K5; and above
all, he will try to play . . . P - QB4 in order to round out

his Queen-side Pawns. Since he has four Pawns to three
in that sector, he will often win by obtaining a passed
Pawn.

To sum up, we may say that White's winning chances
generally reside in attack in the middle game, while
Black's best opportunity lies in effective utilization of his
Queen-side Pawns in an ending. Let us see some practical
samples of the variation:

9. . . .   B - K2

This has been considered Black's best move for many
years. However, (9) . . . B - QB4 deserves consideration; although it has the drawback of postponing the
rounding out of Black's Queen-side Pawns, it has the
positive virtue of posting the KB aggressively. Two possibilities are: (9) . . . B - QB4; (10) QKt - Q2, Castles;
(11) Q - K2, Kt x Kt; (12) B x Kt, B - KKt5; (13) B - KB4,
R - K1 with an interesting struggle for the initiative; or
(9) . . . B - QB4; (10) QKt - Q2, Castles; (11) B - B2,
Kt x KBP°!? (12) R x Kt, P - B3. This venturesome continuation, the consequence of the development of the
Bishop to QB4, leads to a complicated game in which attack and defense are apparently pretty evenly balanced.

BLACK

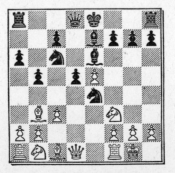

WHITE

There are numerous possibilities for White in this position, but it seems that Black can get a satisfactory game against any of them. Let us·see:

(A) (10) R-K1, Castles; (11) Kt-Q4, Kt x KP ! (Black sacrifices a piece, but gets a very strong attack); (12) P-B3, B-Q3; (13) P x Kt, B-KKt5 followed by (14) . . . Q-R5 with a powerful attack.

Note that (11) . . . Q-Q2 ? would lose a piece: (12) Kt x B and no matter which way Black recaptures, (13) R x Kt ! wins a piece.

(B) (10) QKt-Q2, Castles; (11) Q-K2, Kt-B4; (12) Kt-Q4, Kt x B; (13) QKt x Kt, Q-Q2; (14) Kt x Kt, Q x Kt; (15) B-K3, B-KB4. The position is fairly level. Black's Pawn structure is somewhat weak, but he has two good Bishops.

(C) (10) B-K3, Kt-QR4; (11) Kt-Q4, Castles; (12) Kt-Q2, Kt-B5 and the game promises to become very interesting.

(D) (10) Q-K2, Kt-B4; (11) B-B2, P-Q5 ! and Black stands well.

Thus we see that in all these variations, Black can get a good game so long as he plays alertly and exactly. Unquestionably this is a more difficult line of play than Variation I.

The Steinitz Defense is hardly played nowadays, because it gives Black a cramped game in which the best he can hope for is equality.

1. P-K4	P-K4
2. Kt-KB3	Kt-QB3
3. B-Kt5	P-Q3

This is the basic move of the defense.

4. P - Q4	B - Q2
5. Kt - B3	Kt - B3
6. B x Kt !	B x B
7. Q - Q3 !	

Very strong. As White's KP is amply protected, Black has little choice but to capture; for (7) . . . Q - K2 would constrict Black's game unduly, while (7) . . . Kt - Q2; (8) B - K3 would practically force . . . P x P in view of the threatened (9) P - Q5.

| 7. . . . | P x P |
| 8. Kt x P | B - K2 |

BLACK

WHITE

Black's surrender of the center on his seventh move has greatly increased the scope of White's pieces. There are now at least two very promising ways for White to continue:

(A) (9) B - Kt5, Castles; (10) Castles (Q). White has

genuine attacking chances through the advance of his King-side Pawns. Black is condemned to passivity and his Bishops have very little terrain.

(B) (9) P - QKt3, Castles; (10) B - Kt2, B - Q2; (11) Castles (Q). Again White has fine attacking possibilities, enhanced by the striking power of his QB along the diagonal. He can of course also castle on the King-side with a very good game. Black has little to hope for in either of these eventualities.

These considerations have pointed to a finesse which improves Black's chances:

1. P - K4	P - K4
2. Kt - KB3	Kt - QB3
3. B - Kt5	Kt - B3
4. Castles	

As we have seen (Page 10), this is White's best rejoinder to Black's last move.

4.	P - Q3

Black's subtle transposition of moves has ruled out the possibility of White's castling Queen-side, easing the defense to that extent.

5. P - Q4	B - Q2

Also possible is (5) . . . P x P; (6) Kt x P, B - Q2; (7) Kt - QB3, B - K2; (8) B x Kt, P x B; (9) Q - Q3, Castles; (10) P - QKt3 followed by (11) B - Kt2 and (12) QR - Q1 or QR - K1. White has much the freer game and attacking chances; Black's Bishops have better prospects than in the previous example.

6. Kt - B3	B - K2
7. R - K1	P x P
8. Kt x P	Kt x Kt

Black does best to simplify wherever possible, so as to minimize his lack of terrain. After (8) ... Castles, White could preserve his KB with (9) B - B1! leaving Black with a difficult game.

9. Q x Kt	B x B
10. Kt x B	P - QR3
11. Kt - B3	Castles

Black's command of the board is still painfully restricted, but White's advantage has been reduced. He still has the freer game, more maneuvering space and a clear initiative.

In modern times, still a further refinement was discovered in this defense:

1. P - K4	P - K4
2. Kt - KB3	Kt - QB3
3. B - Kt5	P - QR3
4. B - R4	P - Q3

The Steinitz Defense Deferred. It is an old line of play, but has been cleverly refurbished by modern masters.

BLACK

WHITE

The chief idea of this defense becomes apparent if White proceeds in the most obvious way:

5. P - Q4	P - QKt4 !

Very important. Black does not have this move at his disposal in the regular Steinitz Defense.

6. B - Kt3	Kt x P
7. Kt x Kt	P x Kt
8. B - Q5	

But not (8) Q x P ??, P - QB4; (9) Q - Q5, B - K3; (10) Q - B6 ch, B - Q2 followed by (11) . . . P - B5 winning a piece.

8. . . .	R - Kt1
9. B - B6 ch	

Or (9) Q x P, Kt - B3 and Black has a good game.

9. . . .	B - Q2
10. B x B ch	Q x B

And it is clear that Black has a much better position than in the Steinitz Defense.

However, returning to the Diagram on Page 26, we can see that White has several good lines of play at his disposal:

(A) (5) B x Kt ch, P x B; (6) P - Q4, P - B3. Black plays to hold the center, but his position becomes terribly cramped. This is definitely not a kind of defense to recommend to an inexperienced player. White can continue with (7) B - K3, P - Kt3; (8) Q - Q2, Kt - K2; (9) Kt - B3, B - KKt2; (10) Castles (Q) or (10) B - R6.

(B) (5) P - B3, B - Q2; (6) P - Q4, Kt - B3; (7) Castles. White has a good center and the freer game.

(C) (5) P - B4, B - Q2; 6 Kt - B3, Kt - B3; 7 P - Q4. White has prevented . . . P-QKt4 and has a promising position in the center.

All three lines should preserve a well-defined initiative for White.

In conclusion, the following clever trap in the Ruy Lopez will be of interest as illustrating the dangers of a close defense:

1.	P - K4	P - K4
2.	Kt - KB3	Kt - QB3
3.	B - Kt5	P - Q3
4.	P - Q4	B - Q2
5.	Kt - B3	KKt - K2
6.	B - QB4	

Threatening (7) Kt - KKt5.

6.	. . .	P x P
7.	Kt x P	

Now it seems that Black, in order to keep White's Queen out of KR5, has a good way of developing his KB by means of . . . P-KKt3 and . . . B-Kt2, where the Bishop would certainly have excellent diagonal.

7.	. . .	P - KKt3
8.	B - KKt5	

In order to take possession of the diagonal which Black attempts to occupy.

8.	. . .	B - Kt2
9.	Kt - Q5 !	

Attack and counterattack.

9.	. . .	B x Kt

Anything else would be clearly disadvantageous. Black is of course under the impression that White will continue with (10) Kt x Kt, when (10) . . . B x P would allow Black to get out of danger. But White has a more efficient move at his disposal:

BLACK

WHITE

10. Q x B !

This is very awkward for Black. If now (10) . . . Kt x Q; (11) Kt - B6 ch, K - B1; (12) B - R6 mate. So nothing remains but to castle.

10. . . .	Castles
11. Kt - B6 ch	K - R1
12. Kt - Kt4 ch	Kt x Q
13. B - B6 ch	K - Kt1
14. Kt - R6 mate	

4. Various Replies to 1P-K4

THERE was a time when (1) . . . P-K4 was considered *the* reply to (1) P-K4. In modern chess this state of affairs has been almost completely reversed, and the range of the openings has been widened enormously by the discovery, revival and intensive analysis of many interesting lines of play.

SICILIAN DEFENSE

Many masters consider this line of play the most aggressive reply to (1) P-K4. "Refutations" have been announced periodically, but the defense still maintains its place in the tournament repertoire. True it is that this defense is not for the timid nor for those who feel uneasy in complicated positions.

1. P - K4	P - QB4
2. Kt - KB3	

The "symmetrical" line of play (2) Kt - QB3, Kt - QB3; (3) P - KKt3, P - KKt3; (4) B - Kt2, B - Kt2; (5) KKt - K2, P - K3; (6) Castles, KKt - K2; (7) P - Q3, Kt - Q5 or (5) . . . Kt - B3; (6) Castles, P - Q3; (7) P - Q3, Castles; (8) P - KR3, Kt - K1; (9) B - K3, Kt - Q5 gives Black a good game.

After the text, three outstanding lines deserve consideration.

I

2. . . .	P - Q3

(2) . . . Kt - KB3 can easily lead to early tactical difficulties in the opening, for example (3) P - K5, Kt - Q4; (4) P - Q4, P x P; (5) Q x P, P - K3; (6) B - QB4, Kt - QB3; (7) Q - K4 and Black's game is uncomfortable.

3.	P - Q4	P x P
4.	Kt x P	Kt - KB3
5.	Kt - QB3	P - KKt3

This line of play is known as the Dragon Variation. Black hopes to develop pressure along the diagonal by fianchettoing his KB.

6.	B - K2	B - Kt2
7.	B - K3	Kt - B3
8.	Castles	

An adventurous alternative is (8) Q - Q2 followed by castling QR and the advance of the King-side Pawns. Black counterattacks via the long diagonal and the QB file, with a stormy battle in prospect.

8.	. . .	Castles
9.	Kt - Kt3	B - K3
10.	P - B4	

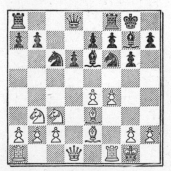

BLACK

WHITE

The coming strategy of both players is clearly outlined. White has a choice of advancing the King-side Pawns or playing for the occupation of Q5, or a combination of both plans.

Black will try to make the power of his KB felt on the long diagonal, and he will operate on the QB file, hoping to be able to plant a Knight at QB5. There is much scope for play by both sides.

II

2.	. . .	P - Q3
3.	P - Q4	

On (3) P - B3, Black has a good reply in (3) . . . Kt - KB3.

3.	. . .	P x P
4.	Kt x P	Kt - KB3
5.	Kt - QB3	P - K3

Here we part company from the Dragon Variation. Black sets up a rather passive Pawn formation, which, however, has great potential power.

6.	B - K2	Kt - B3
7.	Castles	P - QR3
8.	K - R1	Q - B2
9.	Kt - Kt3	B - K2
10.	P - QR4	P - QKt3

White must not be allowed to play P - R5, which would give him a powerful bind on QKt6, cramping Black's game to an intolerable degree.

11.	P - B4	B - Kt2

BLACK

WHITE

A very interesting and difficult position. White will play for a King-side attack by means of P-KKt4 and Q-Kt3 (once Black has castled KR). Black has three sources of counterplay: the QB file, the properly prepared advance of his KP and the possibility of bringing a Knight to QB5. This variation requires precise timing and nicety of judgment. In recent years, White's attack on the King-side has almost invariably proved stronger than Black's defense.

III

2. . . .	P - K3
3. P - Q4	P x P
4. Kt x P	Kt - KB3
5. Kt - QB3	B - Kt5

Apparently formidable, as (6) B - Q3 can be answered by (6) . . . P - K4; (7) Kt - K2, P - Q4 with a good game, while if (6) P - B3 ?, P - Q4 ! and Black has the initiative.

BLACK

WHITE

| 6. P - K5 ! | Kt - Q4 |

If (6) . . . Kt - K5; (7) Q - Kt4 ! is a winning reply.

| 7. Q - Kt4 ! | P - KKt3 |
| 8. B - Q2 | |

White has a strong attack.

FRENCH DEFENSE

This defense is more solid and less venturesome than the Sicilian Defense. Black often gets a cramped game, which gives White good attacking chances or the prospect of exploiting his opponent's constricted position. On the other hand, the solidity of Black's game is a good weapon against premature attacks.

1. P - K4	P - K3
2. P - Q4	P - Q4
3. Kt - QB3	

(3) P x P, P x P gives Black an easy game, as it generally leads to a symmetrical position. The opening of his QB's diagonal is another point in his favor.

The more aggressive (3) P-K5 also has its draw-
backs, as it permits Black to engage in an immediate
counterattack, for example (3) . . . P-QB4; (4) P x P,
Kt-K2 !; (5) Kt-KB3, KKt-B3 followed by . . . Kt-Q2
with a good game; or (4) P-QB3, Kt-QB3; (5) Kt-B3,
Q-Kt3; (6) B-K2, P x P; (7) P x P, KKt-K2; (8)
P-QKt3, Kt-B4; (9) B-Kt2, B-Kt5 ch with a good
initiative against White's somewhat weakened Pawn
center.

After the text, there are three main variations to consider:

I

3. . . .   Kt - KB3

(3) . . . P x P; (4) Kt x P surrenders the center too
readily and leaves White with a fine, free game and good
attacking chances.

4. B - Kt5   B - Kt5

The most aggressive continuation.

5. P - K5

After (5) P x P, Q x P; (6) B x Kt, P x B; (7) Q-Q2,
Q-QR4 Black has a satisfactory game.

5. . . .   P - KR3

Forced.

6. B - Q2   B x Kt
7. P x B   Kt - K5

A fashionable variation which has been the subject of
a great deal of analysis.

8. Q - Kt4

Announcing his intention of prosecuting a fierce attack. The safest reply is (8) . . . K - B1, but it has the disadvantage of keeping the KR out of play for a long time to come.

8. . . .	P - KKt3
9. B - Q3	Kt x B
10. K x Kt	P - QB4
11. P - KR4	Kt - B3
12. R - R3	

BLACK

WHITE

The game promises to become very interesting, as the threat of B x P is already in the air. Black parries the threat and at the same time begins counterplay on the other wing by:

12. . . .	P x P !
13. P x P	Q - Kt3 !

Black has an excellent game. If now (14) B x P?, P x B; (15) Q x P ch, K - Q1; (16) Q - B6 ch, K - B2; (17) Q x R, Q x P ch and wins.

II

3. . . .   Kt - KB3
4. B - Kt5   B - K2

A playable alternative is (4) . . . P x P; (5) Kt x P, B - K2. Black's game is slightly cramped but he has excellent equalizing possibilities.

5. P - K5

In recent years, the old-fashioned (5) B x Kt, B x B; (6) P - K5, B - K2; (7) Q - Kt4 has been revived. White has attacking chances which should be neutralized by Black with proper play.

5. . . .   KKt - Q2
6. P - KR4 !

An interesting attacking line which has led to many brilliant games. The once popular (6) B x B, Q x B; (7) Kt - Kt5 should not worry Black unduly, for example (7) . . . Kt - Kt3; (8) P - QB3, P - QR3; (9) Kt - QR3, P - QB4; (10) Kt - B2, Kt - B5; (11) R - Kt1, P - QKt4 with equal chances.

BLACK

WHITE

It is difficult to suggest a satisfactory continuation for Black. Here are some attempts:

I (6) . . . B x B; (7) P x B, Q x P; (8) Kt - R3, Q - K2; (9) Kt - B4, Kt - B1; (10) Q - Kt4 and White has a dangerous lead in development in return for the Pawn.

II (6) . . . P - QB4; (7) B x B, K x B; (8) P - B4, Kt - QB3; (9) P x P, Kt x BP; (10) Q - Kt4 followed by castling. White has a clear initiative and Black's King is permanently insecure. (7) . . . Q x B is not good because of (8) Kt - Kt5.

III (6) . . . P - KR3; (7) B - K3, P - QB4; (8) Q - Kt4, K - B1; (9) Kt - B3, Kt - QB3; (10) Castles. Here again our judgment must be the same as in the former variation.

IV (6) . . . P - KB3; (7) Q - R5 ch !, P - Kt3; (8) P x P !, Kt x P; (9) Q - K2 or (7) . . . K - B1; (8) P x P, Kt x P; (9) Q - K2. In either event White has the better of it: Black's King is unsafe, and Black has glaring weaknesses in the center.

III

3. . . .   B - Kt5

A fighting defense which usually leads to a tense struggle if White wants to maintain the initiative.

4. P - K5

(4) P x P, P x P frees Black's position and gives him an easy game.

4. . . .   P - QB4
5. P - QR3

White wants to clear the situation at once. A promising alternative is (5) B - Q2, P x P; (6) Kt - Kt5, B x B ch; (7) Q x B, Kt - QB3; (8) Kt - KB3, P - B3; (9) Q - B4, Kt - R3; (10) Kt - Q6 ch with a strong attacking game.

5. . . .	B x Kt ch
6. P x B	Kt - K2
7. P - QR4	QKt - B3
8. Kt - B3	Q - R4
9. B - Q2	P - B5

Black wants to cut down the mobility of the hostile Bishops and to decrease White's attacking chances by blockading the position. There are two good plans open to White: (a) P - Kt3 followed by B - KR3 and if necessary Kt - R4 and P - Kt4 with a view to an eventual P - B5; (b) P - R4 threatening P - R5 - 6; if Black plays . . . P - R4 in reply, White can continue Kt - Kt5, P - B3 and P - Kt4 with a strong game. The position always leads to intricate play with fighting chances for both sides.

CARO-KANN DEFENSE

This is a defense much favored by conservative players who are anxious to curb the ambitions of aggressive opponents. Black sets up a solid attacking position which as a rule leaves few targets for White's attack. In recent years, however, highly promising attempts have been made to give the game a more lively turn. The consensus of opinion is that Black is left with a stodgy game in which he must fight for a draw without having any real winning chances.

1. P - K4	P - QB3
2. P - Q4	P - Q4

As in the French Defense, Black sets up a solid bulwark in the center, but without the disadvantage of blocking the development of his QB. There are now two main lines to be considered.

I

3. P x P

After (3) P - KB3 (the so-called "Fantasy Variation")
it would be foolhardy to allow White a brilliant gambit
attack by means of (3) . . . P x P ?; (4) P x P, P - K4;
(5) Kt - KB3 !, P x P; (6) B - QB4 ! and White has a beautiful attacking position. Instead, Black plays (3) . . .
P - K3; (4) B - K3, Kt - B3; (5) Kt - B3, B - Kt5 or (5) . . .
B - K2 with about even chances.

3. . . .	P x P
4. P - QB4	

This thrust has been analyzed by Russian masters to
good effect. The older line (4) B - Q3, Kt - QB3; (5)
P - QB3 allows Black to obtain a free game with (5) . . .
P - K4, at the cost, to be sure, of an isolated QP.

4. . . .	Kt - KB3
5. Kt - QB3	Kt - B3
6. B - Kt5	P - K3

Inferior is (6) . . . P x P; (7) P - Q5, Kt - K4; (8)
Q - Q4, Kt - Q6 ch; (9) B x Kt, P x B; (10) Kt - B3. Black
is behind in development and his game is disorganized.

7. Kt - B3

(7) P - B5 would be premature, because Black would
be able to counter powerfully later on with . . . P - QKt3
etc.

7. . . .	P x P
8. B x P	B - K2

BLACK

WHITE

The position is approximately even. White has the freer game and attacking chances; Black has pressure on the isolated QP.

II

3. Kt - QB3

After (3) P - K5, B - B4 Black has an easy game: his QB is developed, and he can continue with . . . P - K3 and . . . P - QB4 with a good initiative in the center.

3. . . .	P x P
4. Kt x P	B - B4

(4) . . . Kt - B3; (5) Kt x Kt ch confronts Black with a difficult choice. If he retakes with the KP, he gives White a fine Queen-side majority of Pawns (see the discussion of the Exchange Variation in the Ruy Lopez, P. 17). If he plays (5) . . . KtP x Kt, he has a poor Pawn position and his King-side is broken up. The text-move is safer.

5. Kt - Kt3	B - Kt3
6. P - KR4	P - KR3
7. Kt - B3	Kt - Q2

The plausible alternative (7) . . . P-K3 is effectively answered by (8) Kt-K5 and Black must lose time retreating the QB.

8. B-Q3	B x B
9. Q x B	

White has gained time for development by this exchange; he now intends to castle QR, and Black must follow suit, for if he castled KR, the advanced KRP would be an inviting target for attack.

9. . . .	KKt-B3
10. B-Q2	P-K3
11. Castles QR	Q-B2
12. K-Kt1	Castles
13. P-B4	P-B4
14. B-B3	

BLACK

WHITE

White's position is somewhat freer, and Black's position is rather uncomfortable. He will continue to find himself under constant pressure, without having any possibility of active counterattack. Not an attractive line of play for Black!

ALEKHINE'S DEFENSE

In the days when "hypermodern" chess was fashionable, this defense was a prime favorite. Its basic idea fitted in very well with hypermodern theory: Black lures on White's center Pawns in the hope of demonstrating that such an advance is weakening. At first this policy scored notable successes, in some cases because White played too timidly, in others because White advanced too boldly. But once players with the White pieces learned how to take this opening in their stride, its popularity waned rapidly.

1. P - K4	Kt - KB3
2. P - K5	

(2) P - Q3 is playable but too conservative. (2) Kt - QB3 is feasible, for example (2) . . . P - Q4; (3) P - K5, KKt - Q2; (4) P - K6 !? with an interesting gambit attack; or (2) . . . P - Q4; (3) P x P, Kt x P; (4) B - B4, Kt - Kt3; (5) B - Kt3, P - QB4; (6) P - Q3, Kt - QB3; (7) Q - R5 ! and the absence of Black's KKt from the Kingside may occasion him some difficulty.

2. . . .	Kt - Q4
3. P - Q4	P - Q3
4. Kt - KB3	

White is satisfied with quiet but effective development. The bolder course (4) P - QB4, Kt - Kt3; (5) P - B4 is also quite playable, but it makes heavy demands on White's ingenuity and foresight.

4. . . .	B - Kt5

The most natural development for the Bishop.

5. B - K2	P - K3

Or (5) . . . P-QB3; (6) Kt-Kt5, B x B; 7 Q x B and White's development is more comfortable.

6. Castles	Kt - QB3
7. P - B4	Kt - Kt3
8. P x P	

This exchange is timed to prevent Black from retaking with a piece.

8. . . .	P x P
9. P - QKt3	B - K2
10. B - K3	Castles
11. Kt - B3	

BLACK

WHITE

White's development is freer and more harmonious. Black will lose valuable time trying to find a good square for his KKt—a drawback frequently encountered by him in this opening.

5. Queen's Gambit Declined

SINCE the turn of the century, openings beginning with 1. P - Q4 have played an ever more dominating role in master chess and consequently in the games of all classes of players. It was Dr. Tarrasch who referred to these openings as "the chamber music of chess," thereby paying tribute to their subtlety, their refinement, their hidden beauties . . . and the difficulty of mastering them! The defenses to the Queen's Gambit Declined fall into two fairly distinct family groups, the Orthodox Defense and the Slav Defense.

I. ORTHODOX DEFENSE

1. P - Q4	P - Q4
2. P - QB4	P - K3

Some masters favor the acceptance of the Gambit by (2) . . . P x P. The consensus of opinion is, however, that after (3) Kt - KB3, Kt - KB3; (4) P - K3, P - K3; (5) B x P White has somewhat the freer game because Black's second move has surrendered control of the center rather hurriedly. It should be added, by the way, that attempts to hold the gambit Pawn with such moves as (3) . . . P - QKt4 are inadvisable as a rule, and in the hands of a tyro are quite likely to turn out disastrously.

3. Kt - QB3	Kt - KB3
4. B - Kt5	

A defense which has been very popular in modern times is the Cambridge Springs Variation. The salient moves are (4) . . . QKt-Q2; (5) P-K3, P-B3; (6) Kt-B3, Q-R4. In order to take the sting out of the pin, White generally plays (7) Kt-Q2, with the likely continuation (7) . . . P x P; (8) B x Kt, Kt x B; (9) Kt x P, Q-B2; (10) P-KKt3.

The position is a very interesting one, and not easy to evaluate. Black has two Bishops, but their scope will be very limited. In the coming play, he will strive to open up the game with . . . P-K4 or . . . P-QB4; White, on the other hand, will of course be on the alert to compel Black's game to remain in its cramped state, say by rigorous control of the squares K5 and QB5.

4. . . .	B - K2
5. P - K3	

BLACK

WHITE

Here again we have an interesting possible offshoot: the so-called Lasker Defense. This is seen in its most effective form after the following moves: (5) . . . Castles;

(6) Kt-B3, P-KR3; (7) B-R4, Kt-K5; (8) B x B, Q x B. The underlying idea is to simplify somewhat by exchanges, thereby easing Black's game, which often becomes dangerously constricted. Let us consider some possibilities:

I (9) Kt x Kt, P x Kt; (10) Kt-Q2, P-KB4. Black stands well: he will eventually free himself with . . . P-K4 and he has possibilities of King-side attack.

II (9) B-Q3, Kt x Kt; (10) P x Kt, P x P; (11) B x P, P-QKt3 followed by . . . B-Kt2 and . . . P-QB4 with a comfortable game for Black.

III (9) Q-B2, Kt x Kt; (10) Q x Kt, P x P; (11) B x P, P-QKt3 and Black will eventually free himself with . . . P-QB4.

IV (9) P x P, Kt x Kt; (10) P x Kt, P x P; (11) Q-Kt3, Q-Q3; (12) P-B4, P x P; (13) B x P, Kt-B3; (14) Q-B3, B-Kt5. A good fighting game with chances for both sides.

5. . . .	QKt-Q2
6. Kt-B3	Castles
7. R-B1	

This move is the one now generally played here. Experience has shown that the Rook often exerts considerable power along the QB file. Some masters prefer (7) Q-B2 for the same purpose.

Another line of play which is popular with modern masters is the following: (7) P x P, P x P; (8) Q-B2, P-B3; (9) B-Q3, R-K1; (10) Castles, Kt-B1. White plays to advance his QKtP to Kt5 in an attempt to create weaknesses on Black's Queen-side. Black frees himself with . . . Kt-K5 and is frequently able to obtain good attacking chances on the King-side. The consensus of expert opinion seems to favor White's prospects, but in any

event, this is a variation which calls for expert knowledge
of position play and accurate judgment.

7. . . .   P - B3

Partly to neutralize White's pressure on the QB file, and
partly to support the following exchange maneuver. Black
has the general problem of freeing his game and developing his pieces; he also has the specific task of bringing
out his QB satisfactorily; at present this piece is practically useless. The development of the QB is often Black's
most serious problem in this opening, and many a game
has been lost through failure to solve this problem.

(7) . . . P - QKt3 is now quite out of fashion, as the
weak white squares on Black's Queen-side generally lead
to a strong initiative for White on that wing. A promising
continuation is (8) P x P, P x P; (9) B - Kt5 etc.

8. B - Q3   P x P

It is now or never. Black is determined to free himself.

9. B x P   Kt - Q4
10. B x B   Q x B

BLACK

WHITE

11. Castles

In line with the policy of keeping Black in a cramped position, White might try (11) Kt - K4 here. Black would gradually extricate himself, say by (11) . . . KKt - B3; (12) Kt - Kt3, P - K4; (13) Castles, P x P; (14) Kt - B5, Q - Q1; (15) KKt x P, Kt - K4; (16) B - Kt3, B x Kt; (17) Kt x B, P - KKt3. Black has nothing to fear now, and his Queen-side majority of Pawns should be useful in the endgame.

11. . . .	Kt x Kt
12. R x Kt	P - K4
13. P x P	Kt x P
14. Kt x Kt	

This simplifying line gives Black many chances to go wrong.

14. . . .	Q x Kt
15. P - B4	Q - K5
16. B - Kt3	B - B4
17. Q - R5	P - KKt3
18. Q - R6	QR - Q1

BLACK

WHITE

The position is about even: (19) B - B2, Q - Q4; (20) R - Q1, Q - R4; (21) R x R, Q x R; (22) Q x Q, R x Q etc.

II. SLAV DEFENSE

1. P - Q4	P - Q4
2. P - QB4	P - QB3

The move that gives the defense its name. The basic idea is that in many variations, Black can readily develop his QB.

3. Kt - KB3	Kt - B3
4. Kt - B3	

On (4) P - K3, Black's best course is doubtless (4) . . . B - B4.

BLACK

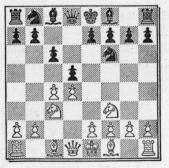

WHITE

4. . . .	P x P

After (4) . . . P - K3; (5) P - K3, QKt - Q2; (6) B - Q3 White has a very comfortable game, for example (6) . . . B - Q3; (7) P - K4, P x KP; (8) Kt x P, Kt x Kt; (9) B x Kt etc.

Another possibility after (6) B - Q3 is (6) . . . P x P;
(7) B x BP, P - QKt4; (8) B - Q3, P - QR3. This is the so-
called Meran Defense, and the latest researches definitely
favor White. A likely continuation is (9) P - K4, P - B4;
(10) P - K5, P x P; (11) Kt x P, Kt x P; (12) Kt x Kt,
P x Kt; (13) Q - B3, B - Kt5 ch; (14) K - K2, QR - Kt1;
(15) Q - Kt3, Q - Q3; (16) Kt - B3, Q x Q; (17) RP x Q
etc. White regains the Pawn and remains with the better
ending.

5. P - QR4

A promising alternative is (5) P - K3, P - QKt4; (6)
P - QR4, P - Kt5; (7) Kt - R2, P - K3; (8) B x P, QKt - Q2;
(9) Castles, B - Kt2; (10) Q - K2, P - B4; (11) R - Q1 !
with an excellent game.

5. . . .	B - B4
6. Kt - K5	QKt - Q2
7. Kt x P (B4)	Q - B2
8. P - KKt3	

A good move. White prepares to fianchetto his KB and
also to develop his QB to B4.

8. . . .	P - K4
9. P x P	Kt x P
10. B - B4	KKt - Q2

Although Black has "freed" himself with . . . P - K4,
his game is still far from easy.

11. B - Kt2	P - B3
12. Castles	R - Q1
13. Q - B1	B - K3
14. Kt - K4 !	

BLACK

WHITE

White's position is definitely preferable. He need not fear (14) . . . B x Kt; (15) Q x B, Kt x Q; (16) B x Q which leaves him with the better game.

Black is embarrassed for a wholly satisfactory continuation. White's pieces bear down strongly on the center and Queen-side, and he can continue with such moves as P - R5, practically paralyzing Black's Queen's wing.

6. *The Indian Defenses*

THIS branch of the openings has been formulated and systematically elaborated only in the last thirty years. Today these openings are the very hallmark of contemporary chess.

KING'S INDIAN DEFENSE

1. P - Q4	Kt - KB3
2. P - QB4	P - KKt3

Black avoids occupying the center with . . . P - Q4. He intends to control the center by fianchettoing the KB and playing . . . P - K4 later on. The drawback to this plan is that White gets control of a substantial amount of terrain.

3. Kt - QB3	B - Kt2
4. P - K4	P - Q3
5. P - KKt3	

Another line of play favored by some leading masters is (5) Kt - B3, Castles; (6) B - K2, QKt - Q2; (7) Castles, P - K4; (8) P - Q5, Kt - B4; (9) Kt - Q2, P - QR4; (10) Q - B2. On the whole, the text continuation is more promising.

5. . . .	Castles
6. B - Kt2	QKt - Q2
7. KKt - K2 !	

An important deviation from the natural development of the KKt to B3. The text does not impede the action of the KB, and in addition it makes possible an early P - B4 in reply to . . . P - K4.

7. . . .   P - K4
8. P - Q5

Beginning a strategy of cramping Black's position. (8) Castles is also quite good, for after (8) . . . P x P; (9) Kt x P, Kt - B4; (10) P - Kt3, R - K1; (11) R - K1 followed by (12) B - Kt2 White's position is manifestly freer and richer in perspectives.

8. . . .   P - QR4

BLACK

WHITE

9. P - QR3 !

White is making preparations to dislodge Black's QKt when it eventually reaches QB4. White can also proceed strongly on the other wing with P - B4. In master play, the results have steadily favored White.

GRUENFELD DEFENSE

This is an offshoot, in more promising form, of the King's Indian Defense.

1. P - Q4	Kt - KB3
2. P - QB4	P - KKt3
3. Kt - QB3	P - Q4

There are a great many possibilities, all of which seem to assure Black a satisfactory game.

I

4. P x P	Kt x P
5. P - K4	Kt x Kt
6. P x Kt	

White has selected the most obvious course, and has built up an imposing center.

BLACK

WHITE

6. . . .	P - QB4 !

The key to Black's strategy. He strikes at White's center by means of the text, in combination with the coming fianchetto of his KB. Incidentally, if Black does not play this move at once, it can be prevented for a long time by B - R3.

7. Kt - B3	B - Kt2
8. B - QB4	Kt - B3
9. B - K3	Castles

Black stands well. He has strong pressure along the diagonal, and is ready to continue with . . . B - Kt5 or . . . Q - R4, possibly preceded by . . . P x P.

II

| 4. B - B4 | B - Kt2 |
| 5. P - K3 | Castles |

Offering a Pawn in return for quick development: 6
P x P, Kt x P; 7 Kt x Kt, Q x Kt; 8 B x P, Kt - B3. Black's
pieces come out very rapidly, and White may soon find
himself in serious difficulties.

BLACK

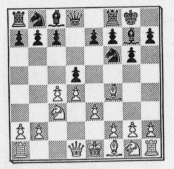

WHITE

6. R - B1

If (6) Kt - B3, P - B4 ! (7) QP x P, Kt - K5 ! or . . .
B - K3 and White's position is exposed to troublesome
threats. The basic idea of . . . P - B4 ! is to try to clear
the diagonal for Black's KB, and also to prepare for . . .
Q - R4, often with a dangerous attack against White's
pinned QKt.

Another possibility is (6) Q - Kt3, P - B4 ! (7) BP x P,
P x P; (8) P x P, QKt - Q2. Black will regain the Pawn
later on with a promising initiative.

6. . . .   P - B4 !

Again Black plays for counterattack. This position is
still the subject of theoretical disputation, but there can

be little doubt that the position is extremely promising
for Black and that White must play with the greatest care
if he is to avoid a permanent disadvantage.

III
4. Q - Kt3

Played to compel Black to make up his mind at once
about how he is to proceed in the center. However, the
move is open to the objection that the Queen is brought
out too early in the game.

4. . . .	P x P
5. Q x BP	B - K3
6. Q - Q3	P - B4 !

In most variations of this opening, Black stands or falls
by the early advance of the QBP. Failure to make this advance in the present variation, for example, would con-
demn Black to lasting inactivity in the face of White's
P - K4 etc.

7. P x P	Kt - R3 !

Whether or not White exchanges Queens, Black has a
tremendous lead in development and should regain the
sacrificed Pawn without much trouble.

IV
4. P - K3

The most conservative possibility at White's disposal;
by the same token, it should not give Black too much
difficulty.

4. . . .	B - Kt2
5. Kt - B3	Castles
6. Q - Kt3	P - B3
7. B - Q2	P - Kt3

(7) . . . Kt - K5 ?; (8) P x P, Kt x Kt; (9) P x P ! loses a Pawn for Black.

8. B - K2	B - Kt2
9. Castles	QKt - Q2
10. KR - Q1	P x P
11. B x P	Kt - K1
12. QR - B1	Kt - Q3
13. B - K2	P - QB4 !

The position is approximately even.

BLACK

WHITE

QUEEN'S INDIAN DEFENSE

This is one of the modern defenses with which Black avoids the symmetrical occupation of the center resulting from the moves (1) P - Q4, P - Q4. In playing the Queen's Indian Defense, Black intends to control the center not by occupation, but by the action of his pieces.

1. P - Q4	Kt - KB3
2. P - QB4	P - K3
3. Kt - KB3	P - QKt3

Black will control K5 by fianchettoing his QB.

4. P - KKt3

This is considered the best antidote to the fianchetto. (4) B - Kt5, B - Kt2; (5) P - K3, B - K2; (6) Kt - B3, Kt - K5 or (5) Kt - B3, B - Kt5 offers Black no difficulties.

4. . . .	B - Kt2
5. B - Kt2	

BLACK

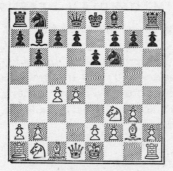

WHITE

5. . . .	B - K2

After (5) . . . B - Kt5 ch; (6) B - Q2, B x B ch; (7) Q x B, O - O; (8) Kt - B3, P - Q3; (9) Q - B2 followed by P - K4, White has an appreciably freer game. In this variation, White's QB does not have much chance to be very effective; hence it is preferable to avoid the exchange.

6. Castles	Castles
7. Kt - B3	Kt - K5

Black continues the fight for control of K5.

| | 8. Q - B2 | Kt x Kt |
| | 9. Q x Kt | |

After (9) P x Kt, the doubled QBP frequently turns out to be a serious weakness.

| | 9. . . . | B - B3 |

Other possibilities are (9) . . . P - Q3, (9) . . . P - QB4 and (9) . . . P - KB4. The position is about even.

NIMZOINDIAN DEFENSE

This is the most complex and the most interesting of all the so-called "irregular" replies to 1 P - Q4. Elaborated by the great modern master Nimzovich, the defense abounds in finesses and calls for strategical understanding of the highest order. Whoever undertakes to play it, must remember above all that it calls for an aggressive spirit at all times.

	1. P - Q4	Kt - KB3
	2. P - QB4	P - K3
	3. Kt - QB3	B - Kt5

Here again we see an avoidance of the orthodox reply (3) . . . P - Q4. White now has a number of continuations at his disposal, which will be considered separately.

I

4. P - QR3

An instinctive reply: White wishes to do away with the pin at the earliest possible moment. In addition, the text confers certain advantages, among them being two Bishops and a solid Pawn formation in the center which augurs well for White's attacking chances.

4. . . .	B x Kt ch
5. P x B	P - B4

Black, on the other hand, is not without consolation: he reasons that concentration on White's weak doubled Pawn should give Black good counterplay.

| 6. P - B3 | |

White is playing to establish a broad Pawn center.

| 6. . . . | Kt - B3 |

The alternative is (6) . . . P - Q4; (7) P - K3, Castles; (8) BP x P, Kt x P and again Black has a good game. This is definitely a variation for aggressive players.

7. P - K4	P - Q3
8. B - K3	P - K4
9. P - Q5	Kt - QR4

BLACK

WHITE

The position is interesting and difficult. White will continue with B - Q3, Kt - K2 - Kt3 followed by P - B4

after castling. Black will play . . . P - QKt3 followed by
. . . B - R3 menacing the weak QBP. A lively struggle is
in prospect.

II

4. Q - B2

A quieter variation, but one which often assures White
an advantage against less than the best play.

4. . . .   P - Q4

The simplest. (4) . . . P - B4 is playable, but it often
results in a weak QP after the reply (5) P x P. If (4)
. . . Kt - B3; (5) Kt - B3, P - Q3; (6) P - QR3, B x Kt ch;
(7) Q x B, P - QR4; (8) P - QKt3, P - Q3; (9) B - Kt2,
Castles; (10) P - Kt3, Q - K2; (11) B - Kt2 and White's
effective Bishops tell in his favor.

5. P x P   Q x P

(5) . . . P x P; (6) B - Kt5 leads to rather a lifeless
game for Black.

6. P - K3   P - B4
7. B - Q2

Apparently best. After (7) P - QR3, B x Kt ch; (8)
P x B, Castles; (9) Kt - B3, P x P; (10) BP x P, P - QKt3
Black has an easy game.

7. . . .   B x Kt
8. B x B

It is difficult to decide whether Black's free position is
satisfactory compensation for White's two Bishops.

BLACK

WHITE

III

4. Q - Kt3   Kt - B3

Also playable is (4) . . . P - B4; (5) P x P, Kt - B3;
(6) Kt - B3, Kt - K5; (7) B - Q2, Kt x QBP; (8) Q - B2,
P - B4; (9) P - QR3, B x Kt; (10) B x B, Castles; (11)
P - KKt3 followed by B - Kt2.

5. Kt - B3   Kt - K5

BLACK

WHITE

Black stands well. He can fortify the position of his KKt with . . . P - B4.

IV

4. P - K3

A quiet line of play, with which White announces that he is content to rely on his skill in the middle game.

4. . . .   P - QKt3

Other playable moves are (4) . . . Kt - B3, (4) . . . P - Q3 or (4) . . . P - B4 or even (4) . . . Castles.

5. B - Q3	B - Kt2
6. P - B3	P - B4
7. Kt - K2	Castles
8. Castles	P - Q4

BLACK

WHITE

Black has at least an even game.

7. Evans Gambit

THIS gambit is constituted by the following moves:—

1. P - K4	P - K4
2. Kt - KB3	Kt - QB3
3. B - B4	B - B4
4. P - QKt4	

BLACK

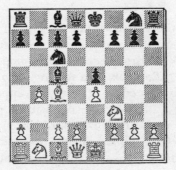

WHITE

There is no necessity for Black to accept the offer of the Pawn. On the contrary, if he retires with his Bishop to Kt3 in reply, he will, as White's last move has in no way furthered his development, gain a small but distinct advantage in position. The play which would then ensue will be of the following character:—

4. . . .	B - Kt3
5. P - QR4	P - QR3
6. P - B3	Kt - B3

7. P - Q3	P - Q3
8. Castles	Kt - K2

soon to be followed by . . . P - B3 and . . . P - Q4.
Black's pieces are all well placed, no matter whether
White castles at his eighth turn to move, or defers that
yet for some time. If White therefore sacrifices a Pawn
by giving the gambit, Black sacrifices the sure prospect
of positional advantage by taking it.

The idea of the gambit is very obvious. We want to
continue, if . . . B x P (or . . . Kt x P), with

5. P - B3

and later on proceed with the advance of the QP, so as
to obtain a very strong center and to open several lines
for the attack of the pieces. The Bishop can retire to
either B4, R4, K2, to his own square, or to Q3, where he
is not so badly placed as at first sight appears. The best
players favor . . . B - R4 or B4, with a preference for
the former. If we retire to B4 the Bishop may be attacked
again by P - Q4, while, on the contrary, . . . B - R4
counteracts that advance. On the other hand, the Bishop
at R4 will take away from the QKt an important point,
from where he might attack the White KB. But taken
all around,

5. . . .	B - R4

seems to be the preferable move.

White has now two formidable continuations:

6. P - Q4

naturally suggests itself first, although it is not of such
lasting effect as another move which we shall consider
later on.

Black will answer

| 6. . . . | P x P |
| 7. Castles | P x P |

The weakest point in Black's camp is the KBP, so we follow up our attack by

8. Q - Kt3

Black can reply with either . . . Q - K2 or . . . Q - B3. From K2 the Q has hardly any move that is not commanded by White's pieces, therefore

| 8. . . . | Q - B3 |
| 9. P - K5 | |

in the expectation of embarrassing Black's development, as neither the QP nor the KBP can advance for the present without being taken, with the effect that all lines are opened up to our pieces.

| 9. . . . | Q - Kt3 |
| 10. Kt x P | KKt - K2 |

BLACK

WHITE

In this position we already see that White's attacking moves are pretty well exhausted. He has only a very unsatisfactory continuation.

11. B - R3

which gives to the Bishop a long file merely in exchange for another one.

This position has been the subject of analysis for many decades, and several variations have been found which seem to leave Black with a comparatively safe K position and a Pawn ahead. None of the continuations given seem to be superior to the one that follows.

11.	B x Kt
12. Q x B	P - QKt3
13. B - Q3	Q - R3

Not . . . Q - R4, as (14) B x Kt, K x B; (15) P - K6 might follow.

14. KR - Q1	B - Kt2

and it is difficult to see in which way White will make good his minus of two Pawns.

This line of play, the so-called Compromised Defense of the Evans Gambit, leads sometimes to very brilliant combinations. Let me give you an instance of this at move 11 of our principle variation.

11.	Castles
12. QR - Q1	KR - K1
13. Kt - K4 !	Q x Kt ?
14. B x P ch	K - B1
15. B - Kt8 !	P - Q4
16. P x P e.p.	Kt x B
17. Kt - Kt5	Q - B4
18. Q - B7 ch !!	Q x Q
19. Kt x P mate	

Instead of (6) P-Q4, the greatest connoisseur of the Evans, Mr. Tchigorin, favored (6) Castles, with the object of maintaining his center. It cannot be doubted that this line of play is more in keeping with the original idea of the gambit.

BLACK

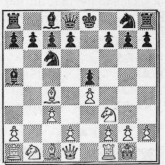

WHITE

Black, in accordance with the principles laid down in Chapter 1, must either play his QP or his KKt. It is usually the best policy when you are subject to a violent attack to move the QP, and when you are the aggressive party to develop your pieces first.

In the position before us

    6. . . .   P-Q3

appears therefore to be the accepted sounder play.

    7. P-Q4   P x P
    8. P x P   B-Kt3

leads to the "normal position" of the Evans. The four Pawns that White has gathered on his K wing against Black's three, exert a considerable amount of pressure on Black's pieces, the more so as Black will be obliged to leave his K on the dangerous side. It is true that Black may establish three Pawns to one on the other wing; but then it will take him a great deal of time to force the fighting on that side, while White's pieces will soon be in direction and ready for assault.

Various continuations have been recommended as best for White; but it seems to me that the old way of playing is as good as any. The line of play usually followed by the old masters is

9.	P - Q5	Kt - R4
10.	B - Kt2	Kt - K2
11.	B - Q3	P - KB3
12.	Kt - B3	Castles

BLACK

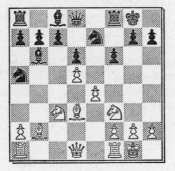

WHITE

It is not my intention to analyze the position by the method usually followed, of simply enumerating all possible variations. Such analysis, unless it is very thorough, I contend, is quite useless. It certainly, as the experience of many centuries indisputably shows, would by no means exclude the possibility of committing grave errors, and it usually puts into obscurity the points of view from which the essential characteristics of the position may be deduced.

Without going into details, this much is certain, either

(*a*) Black will advance his KBP to B4; or,

(*b*) He will initiate an attack on the Q side with . . . P - QB4, . . . P - QR3, . . . B - B2, . . . P - QKt4, etc., or,

(*c*) He will be content to break up White's strong center by . . . P - QB3.

There is, indeed, no other *plan de campagne* to follow.

As regards the first point, it is easily seen that such an advance would not increase the defensive strength of Black's position. It would open the file of the White QB, the point K4 to the White Kts (after the exchange of the Pawns), and probably facilitate the joint attack of the White KBP and KKtP.

(*b*) This was the plan of defense, or rather counterattack, in Anderssen's tierce. White will obtain the advantage in the following manner:

13. K - R1		Kt - Kt3
14. Kt - Q2		P - QB4
15. P - B4		P - QR3
16. Kt - K2		B - B2
17. Kt - KB3		P - Kt4
18. P - B5		Kt - K4
19. Kt - B4		

This will represent pretty accurately the state of affairs ten or twelve moves after the normal position has been arrived at. It takes at least seven moves to bring the Black Pawns to their destination. In the meantime White is free to advance his KKt Pawn in two steps to Kt5, and to open up a pernicious attack against Black's K side.

(*c*) White's policy will be exactly as in (*b*), to advance his KBP. If Black exchanges the QBP against the QP, the KP will retake, and the Black QKt will be unfavorably situated. Black has in this variation practically no chance of winning, in spite of his extra Pawn, while the attack of White is very lasting and dangerous.

It seems then that the normal position will yield to White much better chances of winning than it will to Black.

BLACK

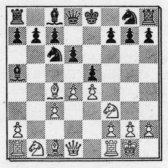

WHITE

If you want to simplify matters, I advise you to play

7. . . .   B - Kt3

at once, with the object of converting your extra material into positional advantage. If then (8) P x P, P x P; (9) Q x Q ch, Kt x Q; (10) Kt x P, Kt - KB3. Black's solid Pawns and good, sound development will make it hard to White to keep up the equilibrium, as his QRP and, more so, the QBP require constant care. If, on the other hand, (8) P x P, P x P; (9) Q - Kt3, Q - B3; (10) B - Q5,

KKt - K2; (11) B - Kt5, Q - Kt3; (12) QB x Kt, K x Kt;
(13) B x Kt, Q x B; (14) Kt x P, Q - K3; (15) Q - R3 ch,
P - B4 or K - B3, with two Bishops, a healthy development of forces and a solid position.

One of the finest games on record was played at a time
when the analysis of the Evans Gambit was not yet far
advanced. It has been named "the evergreen *partie*."

(*Berlin, 1852*)

WHITE	BLACK
A. Anderssen	J. Dufresne
1. P - K4	P - K4
2. Kt - KB3	Kt - QB3
3. B - B4	B - B4
4. P - QKt4	B x P
5. P - B3	B - R4
6. P - Q4	P x P
7. Castles	P - Q6

A now obsolete defense.

8. Q - Kt3	Q - B3
9. P - K5	Q - Kt3
10. B - R3	KKt - K2
11. R - K1	P - QKt4
12. B x P	R - QKt1
13. Q - R4	B - Kt3
14. QKt - Q2	B - Kt2
15. Kt - K4	Q - B4
16. B x P	Q - R4
17. Kt - B6 ch !	P x Kt
18. P x P	R - Kt1

Black: DUFRESNE

White: ANDERSSEN

19. QR - Q1 !!!

One of the most subtle and profound moves on record.

19. . . .	Q x Kt
20. R x Kt ch !!	Kt x R
21. Q x P ch !!	

Grand!

21. . . .	K x Q
22. B - B5 ch	K - K1
23. B - Q7 ch	K - B1
24. B x Kt mate	

If at move 20 Black continues with (20) . . . , K - Q1; (21) R x P ch !, K - B1; (22) R - Q8 ch !, Kt x R; (23) Q - Q7 ch !! and mates in two more moves.

8. King's Bishop's Gambit

T HIS opening is constituted by the following moves:—

1. P - K4	P - K4
2. P - KB4	P x P
3. B - B4	

If I remind you of Rule III you will admit that the development of the B is not in accordance with our fundamental principles. Actually the move of the KKt to B3 would be far stronger, as it leads to a fairly even game, while the KB Gambit should be lost to the first player.

The defense will, before all, disturb the quiet course of White's development, by (3) . . . , Q - R5 ch, to which White is bound to answer with

4. K - B1

According to the principles of development, either the QP or one of the Kts should move. White is threatening to bring forth an enormous force in no more than three moves, to bear upon the center of the board, namely, Kt - KB3, Kt - QB3, P - Q4. Black dare not quietly submit to that, as for the moment his Q is exposed to danger. To keep the White K in his unsound position, to spoil the plan of White, and to aid the quick development of Black's forces, the best policy is the most aggressive one, that is, the one initiated by the sacrifice of the QP.

4. . . .	P - Q4 !
5. B x P	

Now, before anything else is undertaken:

5. . . .   P - KKt4

Our Bishops have two long lines; our Kts have only one
move to make to occupy points of importance, and to add
to the firmness of our position. We can, therefore, spare
the time for this advance of the KKtP, destined to protect
our KBP against all possible attack, and to render the K
side unsafe for White's pieces.

6. Kt - KB3   Q - R4
7. P - KR4   B - Kt2

An excellent reply. The Bishop not only protects the
Rook, but guards the two center points, Q4 (Q5), K5
(K4).

8. P - Q4   P - KR3
9. K - Kt1   Q - Kt3
10. Kt - B3   Kt - K2

So far, everything went all right, because White consistently played for the development of his minor pieces.
Now it becomes apparent that the White QR is awk-
wardly placed, and the QB no less. The K position need
not give any anxiety, but the Q has somehow no good
prospects of serving her cause. At the same time, Black
is quite safe—there is only one weak point in his camp,
the KBP—and any possible attacks of the White minor
pieces in the center are obviated by the clever sacrifice
of the fourth move.

The difficulty of White's Queen-side development will
prove fatal.

BLACK

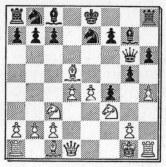

WHITE

11. Q - Q3

preparatory to B - Q2.

  11. . . .   P - QB3
  12. B - Kt3   B - Kt5 !

Here the QB has a splendid position safe of all possible
attack by inferior pieces and with R4 as a safe retreat.

   13. B - Q2   Kt - Q2
   14. K - B2   Castles QR

BLACK

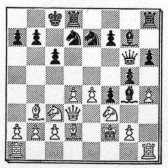

WHITE

All the weakness of the White game becomes now at once apparent. His K and QP are exposed to the most direct attack of the hostile R and Kts, and KB. Try what he may, the day is gone. Black threatens . . . B x Kt and . . . Kt-K4. If (15) Kt-K2, Kt-QB4 wins directly. If (15) P x P, P x P; (16) R x R, B x R the danger is not obviated. If finally (15) Q-B4, B x Kt; (16) P x B, Kt-K4; (17) P x Kt, R x B ch; (18) K-K1, KR-Q1; (19) Q x P, Q x Q; (20) B x Q, B x P; (21) B-Kt3, B x Kt; (22) P x B, Kt-Kt3, followed by Kt-K4, is at least *one* way of obtaining a great advantage.

Let us return to move 11, and vary White's play.

11. P-K5	P-QB3
12. B-K4	B-B4
13. Q-K2	Kt-Q2
14. B x B	Kt x B

White is obliged to undertake some kind of attack, or Black will Castle QR, and the breakdown of White's center will be practically certain.

15. Kt-K4	P-Kt5

Now, at last, this advance is justified, because the QP has lost its protection by the Q.

16. Kt-Q6 ch	K-B1
17. Kt x Kt	P x Kt

and wins a piece or (17) P-R5, P x Kt or (17) Kt-K1, Kt x Kt; (18) P x Kt, B x P ch, and should win.

We must therefore come to the conclusion that the KB gambit is unsound. I will not pretend that there is any right and wrong in Chess from an ethical standpoint, but by what right should White, in an absolutely even position, such as after move 1, when both sides have ad-

vanced P - K4, sacrifice a Pawn, whose recapture is quite
uncertain, and open up his K side to attack? And then
follow up this policy by leaving the check of the Black
Queen open? None whatever! The idea of the gambit, if
it has any justification, can only be to lure Black into
the too violent and hasty pursuit of his attack. If, therefore, we can obtain by sound and consistent play the
superiority of position, common sense triumphs over
trickery, and rightly so.

When the analytical and theoretical knowledge of
Chess was not so far advanced as at the present time,
famous players frequently chose the lively forms of development which are the outcome of gambits. One of
these games, though unsound in the highest degree, has
been of such exceptionally brilliant character that it was
honored by the players of the time with a special name.
We know it as "The Immortal Game." Here its moves
follow:

(*London, 1851*)

WHITE	BLACK
Anderssen	*Kieseritzky*
1. P - K4	P - K4
2. P - KB4	P x P
3. B - B4	Q - R5 ch
4. K - B1	P - QKt4
5. B x P	Kt - KB3
6. Kt - KB3	Q - R3
7. P - Q3	Kt - R4
8. Kt - R4	P - QB3
9. Kt - B5	Q - Kt4
10. P - KKt4	Kt - B3
11. R - Kt1	P x B
12. P - KR4	Q - Kt3

13. P - R5	Q - Kt4
14. Q - B3	Kt - Kt1
15. B x P	Q - B3
16. Kt - B3	B - B4
17. Kt - Q5	

I have not dwelt on the constant violation of principle by Black. The consequence of his imaginative schemes is that none of his pieces are developed; and here White could have smashed Black up by advancing first P - Q4.

17.	Q x P
18. B - Q6 !!	

A fine stroke.

Black: KIESERITZKY

White: ANDERSSEN

18.	Q x R ch
19. K - K2	B x R
20. P - K5 !	

Obstructing the line from QR8 to KKt2. A glorious finish.

20.	Kt - QR3
21. Kt x P ch	K - Q1
22. Q - B6 ch !	Kt x Q
23. B - K7 mate	

9. *The Middle Game*

So far we have considered the first part of a game of Chess, called the opening, and usually embracing about a dozen moves. The object of development is, as we have seen, to get the pieces into action, and to place them on favorable lines, in order to have them at hand when you intend to make them "work." The process of making pieces in Chess do something useful (whatever it may be) has received a special name: it is called the attack. *The attack is that process by means of which you remove obstructions.* That is so in every fight, whether it be a battle, or a fight with swords, or a boxing encounter, this definition will always apply.

Let us compare the game of Chess to some other fight —for instance, to a battle. Two armies opposite each other are attempting to destroy, or at least to frighten, each other. The armies, if about even in numbers, and also as far as favorable position is concerned, will each have a superiority in some quarter which will enable them not only to hold their opponents there in check, but also to drive them out of their position. Three things determine whether an attack should be made, and, if so, in which manner. First of all, the proportion of the attacking force to that directly opposing it in numbers; secondly, the nature of the surroundings; thirdly, the relation of the forces engaged to the rest of the army.

The third consideration will influence the *time* in which the attack must be executed, whether rapidly (if the advent of reserve force must under all circumstances be avoided) or step by step; in other words, it determines whether we should make it our object to economize in time, or in material force at our disposal.

The surroundings will, in part, add to the defensive strength of our opponents, and in part take away from it. Their character will determine which part of the hostile force is exposed to the effect of our weapons, and which is shielded; where we can advance with comparative safety, and which part of the ground we have to traverse rapidly; in other terms, which are weaknesses to be assailed, and which our strong points toward which to advance. The first consideration will tell us whether, after we have gained, by the methodical destruction of the obstacles in our way, a position of advantage, we are able to destroy or drive away the opposing force; or whether the object of our attack, if obtained, is a sufficient compensation for the lives sacrificed. If, in any kind of fight, the rules for attack are laid down, the three things mentioned must be studied.

In Chess the soldiers are the men and the general is the mind of the player. If anything that is subject to the possibility of an attack be a weak point, all men, and especially the King and the heavy pieces (Queen and Rooks), would be such; we shall, however, call a weakness only such pieces, or group of pieces, as in proportion to their importance have a defect in defensive strength, for instance: a Queen, that has only a very limited range of action, or a Pawn that cannot advance nor yet be protected by other Pawns. A weak point is a *square*—not necessarily occupied—which can only be attacked by heavy pieces like the Queen or the Rooks, so that Pawns, Knights and Bishops, or eventually also Rooks, protected by other men, are there quite safe. Our opponent's weak points we shall name strong points, speaking from our point of view. If we can occupy a strong point by one of our pieces, which has from there a large sphere of action, the battle is often half decided in our favor.

Obstructions in Chess are pieces of minor importance which intercept the lines of action of our men. It is, as a rule, easier to remove them when they are hostile men, because we may threaten them by so many of our own pieces that we can finally safely capture them; it is different when, for instance, one of our own Pawns, blocked by one of the Pawns or pieces of the enemy, stands in our way; and worse still when this Pawn is isolated; the only way of removing it by force consists then usually in placing a piece under the protection of this Pawn, and forcing the exchange of that piece.

Let us now consider the initial position. The ultimate object of every attack in Chess is given beforehand—it is the capture by force of the hostile King. For that purpose we must command nine squares, the eight around the King and the one he occupies; we can reduce that number only by driving the King to the edge of the board, or by forcing his own pieces to obstruct his escape. Finally, the checkgiving piece must not be liable to capture, nor must any of the hostile pieces be able to intercept its line of attack. This is the "work to be done," and it is enormous, considering the large amount of force gifted with capacity to capture and obstruct at the enemy's disposal. This task is still made more difficult by the other one which you have to perform—to protect your own King against your opponent's assaults.

The Chess world went about the task thus voluntarily undertaken, and attempted to solve the problem involved by the humanly most direct method; it simply tried it, piling variation on variation, correcting and re-correcting them, for, say, two thousand years. Many beautiful games were played, and startling discoveries made, but the real problem was never solved. And why, may we ask, have for so long a time the exertions of the best brains of the human race continually failed? There is one answer whose cogency is irresistible, an answer whose truth seems to be proved by experience beyond doubt, viz., there *is* no solution, and for this reason the resources on each side are so evenly balanced that the trifling advantage of the first move is not sufficient to force the defense to resignation.

This admitted, we must begin, before entering upon our task, with the supposition that the initial position has been differentiated to such an extent that the win of the game becomes possible to the one or other party. After having granted this much the problem is transformed, and it assumes the following shape: the balance of position and forces has at least been partly disturbed, and to checkmate the King of the inferior force becomes a feasible achievement.

Whether a nearly balanced position allows a forced win to the one or the other party depends usually on the slightest differences, so much so, indeed, that it would be a hopeless undertaking to search for certain rules, or a mathematical formula that would give you its solution without the application of intellectual power in each special case. The question involved is of such a complicated nature that the only way to obtain an answer is to divide the board into parts, to analyze the partial questions by the experimental method, and to finally draw the sum total of all the answers.

Now, given a position in Chess where, on the one wing (for instance, the K side), we have the superiority, on another (the Q side or the center) we may be at a disadvantage, but where, on the whole, our advantage is prevailing, in what manner are we to make capital out of that superiority? The answer depends, of course, on the analysis of the position; but if this analysis is methodical it will greatly acquire clearness and sharpness, and the mental labor required will be reduced to a minimum.

The moves in Chess are of three kinds, they are either

(a) Developing, *i. e.*, bringing new force into play.

(b) Attacking, *i. e.*, making pieces threaten the hostile men, give a check, threaten a checkmate, etc.; in other words, making pieces *do* something, or *work*.

(c) Serving defensive purposes, *i. e.*, giving protection to a weak point, obstructing an important line, etc.; in other words, *undoing* the work of the hostile men.

What kind of move is required is determined by the exigencies of the position. If you have a large superiority of force in a quarter where the enemy has important weaknesses, like the King or the Queen in a bad position, etc., you must assail quickly. Every one of your moves must be intended to do much. Your reserve force must be made useful for the attack with as much gain of time as possible—by attacking, for instance, some weaknesses while on the way—and the reserve forces of the opponent must be kept back, if possible, by obstructions that you can place in their way (think of Morphy's Pawn sacrifices for that purpose). The devices are manifold, but the variations, on account of the many forced moves on the part of the defense, are usually few, and therefore subject to direct analysis. Of such attacks we say that their "pace" is quick.

All the games given (especially the French Defense in Chapter 1) have contained attacks of quick pace. Here follows another.

Black: BAUER

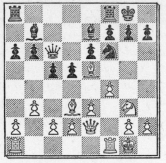

White: DR. LASKER

The game (International Tournament, Amsterdam, 1889) went on

1.	Kt - R5	Kt x Kt
2.	B x P ch !	K x B
3.	Q x Kt ch	K - Kt1
4.	B x P !!	K x B
5.	Q - Kt4 ch	K - R2
6.	R - B3	P - K4
7.	R - R3 ch	Q - R3
8.	R x Q ch	K x R
9.	Q - Q7	B - KB3
10.	Q x B	K - Kt2
11.	R - KB1	QR - Kt1
12.	Q - Q7	KR - Q1
13.	Q - Kt4 ch	K - B1
14.	P x P	B - Kt2
15.	P - K6	R - Kt2
16.	Q - Kt6	P - B3
17.	R x P ch	B x R
18.	Q x B ch	K - K1
19.	Q - R8 ch	K - K2
20.	Q - Kt7 ch and wins.	

When your superiority is not clearly defined, you must be satisfied with attacking at a moderate pace, advancing on your strong points, and methodically creating new ones near your opponent's line of defense. Then the *plan* is everything, and the time a matter of secondary importance. Generally the "pace" of your attack must slacken down the less pronounced your advantage is. A very good player will seldom give you opportunities for violent and short attacks, which require an amount of acting force that is often underrated.

Morphy's games are instructive on these points:

BISHOP'S GAMBIT
(*New York, 1857*)

WHITE	BLACK
Schulten	*Morphy*
1. P - K4	P - K4
2. P - KB4	P x P
3. B - B4	P - Q4
4. P x P	B - Q3
5. Kt - QB3	Kt - KB3
6. P - Q4	Castles
7. KKt - K2	P - B6 !

Black: **MORPHY**

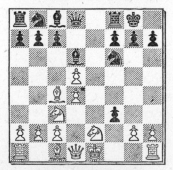

White: **SCHULTEN**

The White King stands in an obstructed file, so Morphy sacrifices his Pawn to prevent the King from castling with safety. It will be remarked that after the sacrifice the defensive power of the White KR and KB Pawn becomes very weak, both of these Pawns being isolated.

8. P x P		Kt - R4
9. P - KR4 ?		

It would have been better to defend by a developing move, such as (9) B - K3, when the following play might ensue: (9) . . . , R - K1; (10) Q - Q2, Q - K2; (11) Kt - K4, B - KB4; (12) B - Q3.

9. . . .	R - K1
10. Kt - K4	

Occupying one of White's *strong points*. It can only be attacked by the KBP or QB, and is therefore an excellent obstruction.

10. . . .	B - Kt6 ch
11. K - Q2	B - Q3
12. K - B3 ?	

Here he unnecessarily exposes himself to new dangers. P - B3 would have provided a safe retreat to the King.

12. . . .	P - QKt4 !

Quickly opening up all the lines on the side which the White King has chosen as refuge.

13. B x P	P - QB3 !

Now he threatens Q - R4 ch., so he indirectly forces White to remove the well-posted Kt from K4.

14. Kt x B	Q x Kt
15. B - R4	B - R3
16. R - K1	Kt - Q2
17. P - Kt3	Kt - Kt3
18. B x P	QR - B1

Every one of Black's pieces has now long open files, in consequence of the energetic attacking manoeuvres of the last six moves.

Black: MORPHY

White: SCHULTEN

19. K - Q2

Black threatened to win a piece by . . . Kt or Q x P. K - Kt2 would have lost immediately on account of (19) . . . , B x Kt; (20) R x B, R x R; (21) Q x R, Kt - R5 ch !, either winning the Queen or checkmating the King on the next move.

19. . . .	R x B !
20. P x R	B x Kt
21. R x B	Q x P ch
22. K - K1	Q - Kt8 ch
23. K - Q2	R - Q1 ch

24. K - B3	Q - B4 ch
25. K - Kt2	Kt - R5 ch

White resigns, for if (26) P x Kt, Q - Kt5 mate; if (26) K - Kt1, Kt - B6 ch, winning first the Queen and then the Rook.

His famous game against Paulsen in the New York Tournament runs as follows:

FOUR KNIGHTS' GAME
(*New York, 1857*)

WHITE	BLACK
Paulsen	*Morphy*
1. P - K4	P - K4
2. Kt - KB3	Kt - QB3
3. Kt - B3	Kt - B3
4. B - Kt5	B - B4
5. Castles	Castles
6. Kt x P	R - K1
7. Kt x Kt	

This capture only develops Black. It would have been quite as good to retire with the Kt to B3 and to follow this up, if (7) . . . Kt x P by (8) P - Q4.

7. . . .	QP x Kt
8. B - B4	P - QKt4
9. B - K2	

The Black Pawns by thus advancing do not, of course, gain in defensive strength, but Black is so far ahead in development that White will never be able to take advantage of that weakness.

9. . . .	Kt x P
10. Kt x Kt	R x Kt

Black: MORPHY

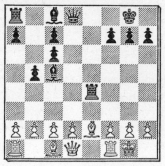

White: PAULSEN

11. B - B3

If here (11) P - QB3, which looks stronger at first sight, then Black will assail the castled King, which for the present is the only support of the KR and KKt Pawn. The game might proceed (11) . . . , Q - R5; (12) P - KKt3, Q - R6; (13) B - B3, R - KR5; (14) P x R, B - Q3; or (12) P - Q4, B - Q3; (13) P - KKt3, Q - R6; (14) P - KB4, B - Q2; (15) B - B3, R - K2; when Black will double his Rooks on the K file and obtain a sound position with many attacking possibilities.

11. . . .   R - K3
12. P - B3 ?

A somewhat elaborate process for so simple an object. First, P - Q3 was the proper play.

12. . . .   Q - Q6 !

This is one of the rare cases in which a heavy piece like the Queen can be used with success for the purpose of obstruction. The Queen cannot be attacked in her present situation by any hostile piece, but exerts a considerable amount of pressure, preventing, for instance, such moves as Q - B2 or B - K2.

13. P - QKt4	B - Kt3
14. P - QR4	P x P
15. Q x P	B - Q2
16. R - R2	

This move may serve as a preparation for Q - B2. White evidently is beginning to feel the restraint which he suffers through the blockade of his QP by the adverse Queen. His plan, however, is frustrated by Black, whose attack has already become ripe for a decisive blow. If (16) Q - R6 instead, Black's best reply seems to be (16) . . . Q - B4; (17) P - Q4, QR - K1; (18) B - K3, P - B4; (19) KtP x P, B x P; (20) Q - R5 ?, R - KKt3, with a winning advantage, for if (21) K - R1, Q x B, (22) P x Q, B - B3, leaves White helpless; therefore White's best would be (20) Q - K2, B - Kt3; (21) B - Kt4, R x B; (22) B x Q, R x Q; (23) B x B, with an even ending

16. . . .	QR - K1

The strongest move for development and simultaneously for attack. Black threatens now Q x R ch.

17. Q - R6

Black: MORPHY

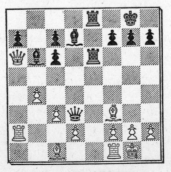

White: PAULSEN

17. . . .   Q x B !!

An effective, surprising, and beautiful coup.

18. P x Q   R - Kt3 ch
19. K - R1   B - R6

Black threatens . . . B - Kt7 ch, followed by . . . B x P
mate. R - Kt1 is no safeguard, as after the exchange of the
Rooks the QR will checkmate him. Nor would (20)
Q - Q3 mend matters, as Black will answer with P - KB4,
and if then (21) Q - B4 ch, K - B1.

20. R - Q1   B - Kt7 ch
21. K - Kt1   QB x P ch
22. K - B1   B - Kt7 ch

He might have decided the issue by R - Kt7, with the
double threat R x P ch, etc., and R x RP.

23. K - Kt1   B - R6 ch
24. K - R1   B x P
25. Q - B1

His only resource.

25. . . .   B x Q
26. R x B   R - K7

Again binding the hostile QP to his post.

27. R - R1   R - R3
28. P - Q4

At last!

28. . . .   B - K6

White resigns, for if (29) B x B, R(R3) x P ch; (30)
K - Kt1, R (K7) - Kt7 mate.

W E T U R N now to games of the post-Morphy era.

RUY LOPEZ
(*Match, 1866*)

WHITE	BLACK
Anderssen	*Steinitz*
1. P - K4	P - K4
2. Kt - KB3	Kt - QB3
3. B - Kt5	Kt - B3
4. P - Q3	P - Q3
5. B x Kt ch	

This exchange is decidedly uncalled for. Black gains thereby an open file, as well as the two Bishops. White has no compensation whatever; for to speak in the early stage of a game of the weakness of a double Pawn or an isolated Pawn for end game purposes is nothing but a chimera.

5. . . .	P x B
6. P - KR3	P - Kt3

Black already has the advantage, and can therefore afford to lose a move for development, which will later on support his plan of attack.

7. Kt - B3	B - KKt2
8. Castles	Castles
9. B - Kt5	P - KR3
10. B - K3	P - B4

An excellent move. Black's plan, as will be seen, is to make the fighting on the K side with his Pawns; he therefor keeps the White QP back, to preserve the obstructions in the center.

Black: STEINITZ

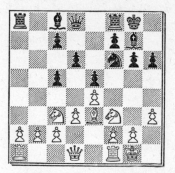

White: ANDERSSEN

11. R - Kt1

It would have been much more to the interest of White to forestall the imminent attack, for instance, by (11) Q - Q2, K - R2; (12) P - KKt4, Kt - Kt1; (13) Kt - R2, P - B4; (14) P - B3.

11. . . .	Kt - K1
12. P - QKt4	P x P
13. R x P	P - QB4
14. R - R4	B - Q2
15. R - R3	P - B4

The White KP, which intercepts the QB's diagonal from QB3, blocks the KP and holds back the QP, dare not be removed. It is, therefore, an excellent object of attack.

16. Q - Kt1	K - R1
17. Q - Kt7	P - QR4
18. R - Kt1	P - R5
19. Q - Q5	Q - B1

White's game suffers for want of design. There is no possible object in all this maneuvering of the heavy pieces. His policy should have been one of defense, which he might conduct with Kt - R2 and P - B3, perhaps successfully.

20. R - Kt6	R - R2

In order to have his Queen free for the following threat, (21) . . . P - KB5; (22) B - Q2, B x P; (23) P x B, Q x P; (24) Kt - R2, P - B6, etc.

21. K - R2	P - KB5
22. B - Q2	P - Kt4
23. Q - B4	Q - Q1
24. R - Kt1	Kt - B3
25. K - Kt1	Kt - R2

The RP will advance and then the KtP, to be followed by . . . Kt - Kt4, where the Kt will have in conjunction with his advanced Pawns a commanding sway. Mark how carefully all this is prepared. No strong point is left to the White party in the rear of the Black Pawns, nor in front of them, during the whole of the tedious process.

26. K - B1	P - R4
27. Kt - Kt1	P - Kt5
28. P x P	P x P
29. P - B3	Q - R5
30. Kt - Q1	Kt - Kt4
31. B - K1	Q - R7

Black: STEINITZ

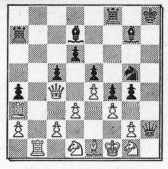

White: ANDERSSEN

Here we have the beau ideal of the concluding stages of a King side attack supported by a chain of Pawns. If P x P, all the lines are opened by . . . P - B6 with tremendous effect. White cannot much improve his position, as his pieces have no space to execute any movements. So Black has any amount of time to prepare the finishing stroke.

32.	P - Q4	P x BP
33.	KtP x P	Kt - R6
34.	B - B2	Kt x Kt
35.	P x BP	

Of course, if (35) B x Kt, B - R6 ch wins.

35.	. . . .	Q - R6 ch
36.	K - K1	

or (36) K x Kt, B - KB3 the White King being quite help-less.

36.	. . . .	Kt x P ch
37.	R x Kt	Q x R

and Black won easily a few moves later.

*Do not overlook how the apparently unimportant sixth
move on the part of White was the real reason of all the
trouble that he had to undergo later.*

SCOTCH GAME
(*Match, 1886*)

WHITE	BLACK
Steinitz	*Zukertort*
1. P - K4	P - K4
2. Kt - KB3	Kt - QB3
3. P - Q4	P x P
4. Kt x P	Kt - B3

According to our rules this should be the strongest
reply. It certainly is a move that answers all purposes.

5. Kt - QB3	B - Kt5
6. Kt x Kt	KtP x Kt
7. B - Q3	P - Q4
8. P x P	P x P
9. Castles	Castles
10. B - KKt5	P - B3
11. Kt - K2	B - Q3
12. Kt - Kt3	

The Kt occupies a square which White would do better
to reserve for the Bishop. (12) Kt - Q4 seems therefore
preferable.

12. . . .	P - KR3
13. B - Q2	

After the development of the Knight to Kt3, this retreat
is inevitable.

BLACK

WHITE

| *13.* . . . | Kt - Kt5 |

Excellent! Black now threatens Q - R5. If White replies by (14) P - KR3, then Kt x P; (14) K x Kt, Q - R5; (15) Q - B3, P - KB4 winning.

14. B - K2	Q - R5
15. B x Kt	B x B
16. Q - B1	B - K7

What he purposes with this is not very clear. He ought to strike hard while White is yet behind in the development of his Rooks, thus: (16) . . ., P - KB4; (17) B - B4, B - B4; (18) R - K1, P - KKt4; (19) B - K3, B x B; (20) P x B, P - B5, with an excellent attack; or even (16) . . . B - Q2 will give him a lasting attack, difficult to meet.

17. R - K1	B - R3
18. B - B3	P - KB4
19. R - K6	QR - Q1
20. Q - Q2	

Now he threatens Q - Q4, or the doubling of the Rooks on the open file; but mark how finely Black frustrates all this.

20. . . .	P - Q5
21. B - R5	

Of course he cannot take the Pawn without losing a piece.

21. . . .	R - Q2
22. R x B	R x R
23. B - Kt4	Q - B3
24. R - Q1	R - Q4
25. B x R	Q x B
26. Kt - R5	Q - K1
27. Kt - B4	R - K4

Black is first to take the open file—a great advantage, which White should not have yielded at move 26.

28. P - KR4	P - B4
29. P - R5	

Black: ZUKERTORT

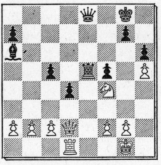

White: STEINITZ

This maneuver with the RP, which is to make the position of the Kt unassailable, is misplaced. The RP exposes itself only to the attack of the Bishop.

29. . . .	R - K5
30. P - QB3	

This unnecessary advance is the principal reason for the speedy conclusion that follows. Black's play from now to the end is admirably consistent and strong.

30. . . .	Q - Kt1
31. P - KKt3	Q - K4
32. Kt - Kt6	Q - Q3
33. Kt - B4	P - Q6
34. P - Kt3	

If (34) Kt x P, B x Kt; (35) Q x B, R - K8 ch wins the Rook or Queen.

34. . . .	P - B5
35. R - Kt1	K - R2
36. K - R2	Q - QKt3

First rate; he now threatens R - K7.

37. K - Kt1	B - Kt2
38. R - Kt2	Q - QB3
39. P - B3	Q - B4 ch
40. Q - B2	R - K8 ch
41. K - R2	

or (41) K - Kt2, R - K6.

41. . . .	Q x Q ch
42. R x Q	B x P

Decisive. The QP must now win.

43. P - KKt4	B - K7

and Black won a few moves later.

If we glance critically over the games given, we find two rules confirmed:

(I) Don't attack unless you have some tangible superiority, either in the stronger working of your pieces, or in longer reach.

Corollary: If you do, the reaction will place your army in a critical position, and the inevitable counter-attack will find you in disorder.

(II) Let it be the first object of your attack to create strong points as near your opponent's camp as possible, and occupy them with pieces which have from there a large field of action.

Corollary: Try to force your opponent's Pawns to advance on the side where you attack.

RUY LOPEZ
(*Dresden, 1892*)

WHITE	BLACK
Dr. Noa	*Dr. Tarrasch*
1. P - K4	P - K4
2. Kt - KB3	Kt - QB3
3. B - Kt5	Kt - B3
4. Castles	Kt x P
5. R - K1	Kt - Q3
6. B - R4	B - K2
7. Kt x P	Kt x Kt
8. R x Kt	Castles

Now Black's development is excellent, and the Pawn position unassailable.

9. P - Q4	Kt - B5
10. R - K1	P - Q4
11. P - QB3	

White has no time for such a move. (11) B - Kt3, Kt - R4; (12) Kt - B3, Kt x B; (13) RP x B, B - Q3; (14) Q - B3, P - QB3; (15) B - B4, is a sounder line of play.

11. . . .	B - KB4

Immediately bearing down on the weak points of White, Q3, QB2.

12. Kt - Q2	Kt x Kt
13. B x Kt	B Q3
14. Q - R5	

This maneuver has not much point. (14) B - B2 is more to the purpose.

14. . . .	B - Kt3
15. Q - R3	P - QB3

From here to the end Black's play is simply classical. Mark now how finely Black will combine the advantage resulting from the weak position of the White Queen, the slight weakness contained in the loose and ineffective positions of the White Bishops, his own strongly posted QB, and the lack of protection of the White QKtP for a highly logical and successful attack.

16. R - K2	Q - Kt3
17. B - Kt3	P - QR4

Capital! Developing the QR, dislodging the obstruction, and keeping the QKtP in its unsafe position.

18. B - K3	P - R5
19. B - Q1	KR - K1
20. R - B1	P - KB4

Grand! He forces White to advance either the KKtP or KBP. In the latter case K5 becomes a very strong point, in the former the Q is obstructed, and the P position weakened.

21. P - KB4	R - K2
22. QR - B2	QR - K1
23. B - B1	Q - Kt4

preventing Q - Q3, and again bearing down on the central weak points of the White game.

24.	Q - B3	Q - B5
25.	P - QR3	R - K5
26.	P - KKt3	P - B4

To get his reserve force, the KB, into play.

Black: TARRASCH

White: NOA

27.	R x R	BP x R
28.	Q - K3	Q - Q6
29.	Q x Q	P x Q
30.	R - B2	P - Kt4
31.	B - Q2	B - K2
32.	P - B5	B - B2
33.	R - B1	P x P
34.	P x P	B - B3
35.	B - QB3	R - K5
36.	B - B3	B x P ch
37.	K - Kt2 ?	

A mistake. (37) B x B, R x B; (38) R - Q1 is by far the preferable policy.

37.		B x B

Energetic and decisive, but not very difficult to foresee.

38. B x R	P x B
39. P x B	B - Kt6

and White resigns, for after (40) K - B2, P - Q7; (41) K - K2, B - B5 ch he will lose his Rook.

QUEEN'S GAMBIT DECLINED

(*Match, 1892*)

WHITE	BLACK
Lasker	*Blackburne*
1. P - Q4	P - Q4
2. Kt - KB3	Kt - KB3
3. P - B4	P - K3
4. Kt - B3	QKt - Q2
5. B - B4	P - B3

On account of the last move which is more or less forced (not to allow Kt - QKt5) the development chosen by Black is not advisable

6. P - K3	Kt - R4
7. B - Kt5	B - K2
8. B x B	Q x B
9. B - Q3	P - KKt3
10. Q - K2	Castles
11. Castles KR	P - KB4

Attacks on the K side in this opening have usually little hope of success. An inspection of the position will show that the K side does not present weaknesses that could be assailed. The fight is, therefore, in the center and on the Q side.

12. KR - Q1	QKt - B3
13. QR - B1	B - Q2
14. Kt - K5	B - K1
15. Q - B2	

Black has, with his 11th move, stopped the advance of
the White KP. The White Q is therefore now available for
the Q's wing.

15. . . .	R - Q1
16. P - QR3	Kt - Q2
17. Kt - B3	Kt - Kt2
18. R - K1	

White intends a Q side attack; and, therefore, first
makes preparations to take advantage of any forward
movement that Black might undertake on the K side, beginning with P - B5.

Black: **BLACKBURNE**

White: **LASKER**

18. . . .	Kt - B3
19. P - QKt4	Kt - K5
20. Kt - K5	Kt x Kt
21. Q x Kt	Kt - R4

22. P - QR4	Kt - B3
23. P - Kt5	Kt - Q2
24. Kt - B3	P x BP

White threatened now P - B5, followed by P - R5 and
P - R6, to establish a dangerous passed Pawn at B5.

25. Q x P	Kt - Kt3
26. Q - Kt3	P x P
27. P x P	B - B2
28. Kt - K5	R - B1
29. R - R1	

The object of White's attack was to keep the QRP back,
which is now indefensible.

29. . . .	R - R1
30. R - K2	KR - B1
31. KR - R2	Q - B2
32. P - Kt3	Q - B6
33. Q x Q	R x Q
34. R x P	R x R
35. R x R	R - B2

The attack has now succeeded. White has the advantage
of a Pawn plus on the K side. What remains is to convert
this into positional superiority—not an easy process, as
still there are hardly any assailable points in the Black
camp.

36. K - B1	B - K1
37. K - K2	K - B1
38. K - Q2	K - K2
39. R - R3	K - Q3
40. P - B3	R - B1
41. P - K4	R - B2
42. R - R1	R - B1

43. P - R4	R - B2
44. R - QKt1	R - B1
45. K - K3	K - K2
46. P - R5	

The decisive maneuver. If the P is taken, the two isolated
RPs will be a splendid object of attack, well worth the
sacrifice.

46. . . .	K - B3
47. RP x P	RP x P
48. R - KR1	K - Kt2

Here, after some maneuvers to complete the third
hour (we played eighteen moves an hour), the game
went on at move 55, the position being unchanged.

55. P - Kt4	P x KtP
56. P x P	R - R1
57. P - Kt5	

Threatening Kt - Kt4 - B6 etc.

57. . . .	R - R6
58. K - Q2	R - R7 ch.
59. K - K3	R - R6
60. K - B4	Kt - Q2
61. B - B4	Kt - B1
62. R - QB1	

The finishing stroke. The Rook will now enter *via* B7
into the Black camp.

62. . . .	R - R4
63. B - Q3	B x P
64. R - B5	

and White won easily.

11. *Defensive Play*

IF THE attack is the process through which obstructions are brought out of the way, the defense is the art of strengthening them, of giving firmness to your position, and of averting the blow directed against you. When your position is not inferior to that of your opponent, and he nevertheless makes preparations to attack you, disregard them altogether, develop reserve forces, avoid his attack by the slightest defensive movement possible (like a first-rate boxer, who in the nick of time and with an almost imperceptible movement evades the blow), and institute a quick counter-action. When, however, you have been unfortunate enough to compromise yourself, to give your opponent an undeniable reason for and tangible object of attack (which may occur to the best and most cautious player as the result of an unsuccessful attack), you have to act very differently.

Also here common sense tells us exactly how to proceed. Every position will comprise points which are exposed to the action of the hostile forces and other points which are well guarded. An attack will direct itself in the first instance against your weakest points—for instance, against the KRP and KKtP after Castling, or against a Kt at B3, etc. You will, therefore, first of all, evacuate these points if they are occupied by men of great importance, the Queen or Rook, for instance, and also frequently a Knight and a Bishop; secondly, you will have to give them support; place the support in points which are not easily accessible by the enemy. The rest of your army is best employed in engaging the reserve force of the enemy—that is, such force which it will take him time and labor to utilize for the purposes of his attack.

The object of your opponent's attack is, generally speaking, to change the position of your men in a certain quarter by force. Abstain from changing it voluntarily, except for most forcible reasons. This is where most Chess players fail. In order, for instance, to avoid the approach of a Kt or Bishop to Kt5, they advance the RP to R3, losing a move, and besides, as a general rule, impairing the strength for purposes of defense of the chain of Pawns on the wing; or they advance the KKt Pawn to Kt3, to drive a Kt away posted at KB4, which, however well placed, is usually not half as dangerous as this move; or they retire a piece, because it may be driven away. Wait with all such moves until your antagonist has expended some time, material position, etc.—well, call it, taken altogether, some of the "power" at his disposal—on them.

For the rest your defensive movements must, of course, be subservient to the objects of the enemy's attack. You may, therefore, invert the rules for attack; let it be your object to prevent your opponent from creating strong points very near your line of defense. That comprises everything, as we shall see in the following instances.

SCOTCH GAME

1. P - K4	P - K4
2. Kt - KB3	Kt - QB3
3. P - Q4	P x P
4. Kt x P	Kt - KB3
5. Kt x Kt	KtP x Kt
6. B - Q3	P - Q4
7. P - K5	

Black has followed up to this point the rules of development. He has given to White no object of attack, none of his pieces being in a weak position. White's attacking maneuver is, therefore, premature.

7. . . .		Kt - Kt5
8. Castles		B - QB4
9. P - KR3		

BLACK

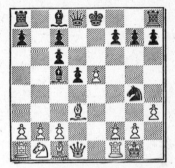

WHITE

Now follows a clever stroke, which shows how unsound all White's play has been.

9. . . .		Kt x KP
10. R - K1		Q - B3
11. Q - K2		Castles
12. Q x Kt		Q x P ch
13. K - R1		B x RP
14. P x B		Q - B6 ch
15. K - R2		B - Q3

and Black wins.

MAX LANGE ATTACK

1. P - K4	P - K4
2. Kt - KB3	Kt - QB3
3. P - Q4	P x P
4. B - B4	B - B4
5. Castles	Kt - B3

(5) . . . , P - Q3 would be more in conformity with our rules. The text move is slightly inferior, and gives White the opportunity to a violent onslaught, which, however, in the face of Black's splendid development, fails against, the best line of defense.

6. P - K5	P - Q4

The right reply. To remove the Kt would be vastly inferior. If, for instance, (6) . . ., Kt - K5; (7) B - Q5 would disorganize Black's game; and if (6) . . ., Kt - Kt5; (7) B x P ch, K x B; (8) Kt - Kt5 ch, might follow.

7. P x Kt	P x B
8. R - K1ch	B - K3
9. Kt - Kt5	Q - Q4

Not Q - Q2, as (10) Kt x B, P x Kt; (11) Q - R5 ch, would allow White to gain the KB.

10. Kt - QB3	Q - B4
11. P - KKt4	Q - Kt3

Black must not take the KBP, as White would answer with (12) Kt - Q5, Q - Q1; (13) R x B ch, P x R; (14) Kt x P. Now Black threatens to Castle Q side with a magnificent game, as White through his attacking maneuvers has vastly impaired the solidity of his position.

12. QKt - K4	B - Kt3
13. P - B4	Castles QR
14. P - B5	B x P
15. P x B	Q x P(B4)

At last White has recouped himself in material, but at what an expense! He is three Pawns behind, his King is in a totally unsafe position, his enemy is brilliantly developed, and the QP and QBP, far advanced and well protected, are ready for decisive action whenever the slightest opportunity is offered. All this for a minor piece. Note that if White now continues (16) Kt x BP, Black has a winning reply in (16) . . . Q - Kt3 ch.

16. P x P	KR - K1
17. Kt - Kt3	P - Q6 ch
18. B - K3	B x B ch
19. R x B	Q - B4

or . . . Q x Kt winning. Similar conclusions follow in any variations that White may choose after move 13. Therefore let us go back to that position, and vary the attack.

13. Kt x BP

A bold sacrifice, to maintain the attack. If . . . K or Q takes Kt, Kt - Kt5 will regain the piece, with an excellent position. If . . . B x Kt, White must be satisfied with driving the King into a somewhat exposed position by (14) P x P, Q x P; (15) Kt - B6 ch, K - Q; (16) Q - B3, with good attacking possibilities against the exposed King. Black, however, has just as bold a reply, which utterly turns the tables and gives him the attack against the weakened K side of White.

BLACK

WHITE

13. . . .   Castles KR

Now, at once, all of the White pieces become badly placed, and must speedily return to their camp. The tide turns and the reaction sets in.

14. KKt - Kt5	B - Q4
15. P x P	KR - K1
16. Kt - Kt3	P - KR3
17. Kt - R3	Kt - K4

and Black should win; or, perhaps more effectively,

17. . . .	R x R ch
18. Q x R	R - K1
19. Q - Q1	Kt - K4
20. Kt - B4	Q - QB3

with a brilliant attack.

1. P - K4	P - K4
2. Kt - KB3	Kt - QB3
3. P - B3	

The Ponziani Opening. I cannot recommend it on account of the questionable early advance of the QB Pawn.

3. . . .	P - Q4

An excellent answer. By his third move White has weakened the square Q3; so Black tries to open the Q file, to get possession of that very important point.

4. Q - R4	P x P
5. Kt x P	Q - Q4
6. B - Kt5	Kt - K2
7. P - KB4	

This is the move given by Staunton. It is intended to keep up the attack, which by the exchange of the minor pieces would be utterly lost. White threatens now B - B4, and Staunton lets Black, therefore, reply by P x P *e.p.* A fine Liverpool player, looking at the position with the instinct of a true Chess player, thought that there must be, against such precipitate attack as White has undertaken, a better reply. And this is how he proved his point:

7. . . .	B - Q2
8. Kt x B	K x Kt
9. Castles	Kt - B4

B L A C K

W H I T E

Black has by far the better development, and now threatens B - B4 ch.

10.	P - QKt4	P - QR4
11.	K - R1	P x P !!
12.	B x Kt ch	P x B
13.	Q x R	B - B4 !!
14.	Q x R	Kt - Kt6 ch !
15.	P x Kt	Q - R4 mate

FRENCH DEFENSE

(*Bradford, 1888*)

WHITE	BLACK
Blackburne	*Burn*
1. P - K4	P - K3
2. P - Q4	P - Q4
3. Kt - QB3	Kt - KB3
4. P - K5	KKt - Q2
5. P - B4	P - QB4
6. P x P	B x P
7. Q - Kt4	Castles
8. B - Q3	P - B4
9. Q - R3	Kt - QB3
10. Kt - B3	R - K1

Black is evidently preparing his K side for a long siege. His last move answers that purpose excellently. The Rook vacates the square KB1 for the Kt, which is there quite secure, and gives his support to the weakest point, the KRP, besides to K3 and to Kt3, and is always ready to obstruct the KKt file.

11.	P - KKt4	P - KKt3
12.	P - R3	

One of those harmless looking moves, to prevent something that really is no threat at all. These superfluous defensive moves spoil many a game. Why not at once Q - Kt3, and then a vigorous advance of the KRP?

12. . . .	P - QR3
13. B - Q2	P - QKt4
14. P x P	KtP x P
15. Castles QR	Kt - B1
16. KR - Kt1 ch	

A bold and promising sacrifice, which yields a violent attack very difficult to meet.

16. . . .	B x R
17. R x B ch	Kt - Kt3
18. Kt - K2	R - R2

Again an excellent defensive maneuver. The Rook protects several of the weakest points, and can be used as a means of obstructing the open KKt file.

19. Kt - Kt3	KR - K2
20. Kt - R5	K - R1
21. Kt - B6	R - KKt2
22. Q - R6	Kt - B1
23. Kt - Kt5	

Black: BURN

White: BLACKBURNE

Black is practically out of danger, but must yet play very carefully. White intends now to continue with (24) Q x R ch !, R x Q; (25) Kt - B7 ch !, R x Kt; (26) R - Kt8 mate.

23. . . .	R - Kt3
24. Q - R5	QR - KKt2
25. R - Kt3	Q - K2 ?

A careless move, allowing (26) Kt(5) x RP !, R x Kt; (27) R x R ! and wins. Luckily, White also overlooks this possibility.

26. B - K2 ?	R x Kt(B3) !

Vigorous and decisive.

27. P x R	Q x BP
28. R - QB3	B - Q2
29. Kt - B3	K - Kt1

White threatened R x Kt, followed by B - B3.

30. Q - R3	Kt - Kt3
31. Q - R6	Q - K2
32. R x Kt	B x R

A last attempt to neutralize Black's material superiority by attack.

33. B - B3	R - B2
34. Kt - Kt5	Kt x P
35. Kt x R	Kt x B ch
36. K - Q2	Kt x B

and Black won after a few more moves.

Black: STEINITZ

White: **LASKER**

The annexed position occurred in my first match with Steinitz; White to move. I played somewhat hastily.

1. R - B1

being under the impression that Kt x R would lead to a draw by perpetual check. This is, however (as, I believe, first pointed out by Tchigorin), not the case, *e.g.*, (1) Kt x R, Q - Kt8 ch; (2) K - Q2, Q x P ch; (3) K - Q1, Q - Kt6 ch; (4) K - K2, Q - B5 ch; (5) K - K1!, Q x P ch; (6) B - Q2, Q - R8 ch; (7) K - K2, and White should win easily.

1. . . .	Q - B7
2. B - Q2	R - K2
3. Kt - K6	Q x P ch

Here White must be extremely careful in selecting his reply. If he plays the plausible (4) K - Q1, Q - Kt8 ch; (5) B - B1, Kt - Q6; (6) Q x QP, Kt x P ch; (7) K - K2, Q - K5 ch; (8) B - K3, Q x B ch !, equalizing the material forces, and with good chances for a draw.

4. Q - K3	Q x KKtP

Now follows a very important maneuver, the key to White's defense.

5. P - Kt3

If (5) Q - K2 instead, Black will answer by . . . Q - Q4, and have all the Q side at his own disposal.

5. . . .   R - K1

To take the RP would not be sufficient to keep the balance of forces; White would reply with K - Q1 or P - Kt5, and very soon be able to assume the attack.

6. Q - K2   Q - R6

The first symptom of the gradual exhaustion of Black's attack. The Q would be better posted somewhere on the Q side; but . . . Q - Q4 is not playable, as P - B4 would now force the exchange of Queens.

7. K - Q1   R - QR1
8. R - B2   R - R7

Black's pieces are well placed, but they do not threaten anything.

9. P - Kt5   P - B4
10. Kt x P   P - Q4
11. K - B1

White threatens to drive the Rook away, in order to bring matters speedily to a climax.

11. . . .   Q - Q6

(11) . . . P - B5 would be answered by (12) P x P, (11) . . . Kt - Q6 ch by K - Kt1; and the resulting exchanges leave White always in the possession of his advantage.

12. Q x Q	Kt x Q ch
13. K - Kt1	R - Kt7 ch
14. K - R1	R x P
15. R - B3	

and White won the ending.

Black: LASKER

White: STEINITZ

This diagram shows the state of the game No. 18, at move 33, White to play, of my first match with Steinitz. I recommend a careful study of this position, in which White can keep the balance only by a very ingenious defensive maneuver. The question concerns *only* the next move of White. Black threatens (1) . . . , Kt x P ch; (2) Kt x Kt, B x Kt; (3) Q x B, Q - K8 ch, winning.

How is White to save his game?

If (1) R - B2, R x R; (2) B x R, Q - QB3; (3) K - Kt2, Kt x P; (4) Kt x Kt, Kt - K4, will regain the piece and keep the Pawn plus.

If (1) R - K2, R - B8; (2) B - B2, Q - Q4; (3) Kt - K3, Q x BP, or else (3) R - Q2, Kt x P ch; (4) Kt x Kt, Q x Kt; (5) Q x Q, B x Q; (6) R x Kt, R x B, should win. (1)

Kt - K3 may be answered by (1) . . ., R - B8; (2) R - Q1, Kt x P ch; (3) Kt x Kt, R x R ch; (4) Kt x R, Q - Q4, again remaining a Pawn ahead, with at least an even position.

If (1) K - Kt2, Kt x P; (2) Kt x Kt, Kt - K4; (3) R - Q3, R - B8; (4) R - Q8 ch, K - Kt2; (5) Q - R7, Q - B3, will yield an irresistible attack to the second player.

The move actually made, and the only one to save the game (which ended in a draw) was (1) K - B1! against which Black must play very cautiously not to be at a disadvantage; any too violent attack will fail.

You will have sometimes to look very deep into the position to find a good move for the defense. But this much, I believe, I can promise you, that if you follow the rules laid down you will not search in vain. If you will seek, you will find, no matter how dangerous the attack may look.

12. *The End Game*

WHEN both parties through the struggles of the middle game have held their own, when by the exertions undergone in attack and defense the material forces on both sides have become decimated, and direct attacks on the King have consequently lost any chance of success, the game enters upon a new stage, differing in many points from those preceding it. Of this part of the game, called the end game, it is a characteristic that the King—hitherto the direct or indirect object of attack on the part of your opponent—over whose safety you anxiously watched, and whose power was limited to the protection of a few Pawns needed for his own security, now becomes a powerful weapon of offense and aggression in your hands.

When the game enters this last stage, the general rules for attack and defense are not changed in any particular. Weaknesses will be represented principally by Pawns, which are blocked, or cannot advance for some other reason, and which, besides, cannot be defended by other Pawns. Here again the attack will direct itself against the weaknesses. Our weak points will be such as are open to the enemy's men or King, and not commanded by any of our own men nor by our King; our opponent's chief attack will be directed toward those strong points, and will attempt to create new ones as near the hostile weaknesses as it has the power to do. Here also the attacking party needs, for success, a superiority of some kind. But, in combination with all this, two new factors enter into the end game which give it its peculiar character.

The first is based on the greater facility acquired (in consequence of the exhaustion of the material forces) to lead your passed Pawns to Queen. For that purpose there are never more than five separate moves required, and often less. If the line where the Pawn advances consists entirely of strong points, the enemy will be obliged to engage one of his men, perhaps his King, whose function it will be to command one of these points or to obstruct that line. Points and lines through which the hostile men prevent the advance of the passed Pawn may be called *points of vantage* in regard to it. The game will very often then present a fight for the command of these points or lines of advance, which may be intercepted by our men, or from which the hostile forces may be driven back. On the other hand, being quite satisfied with the result that part of the hostile army is engaged in watching our passed Pawn, we may undertake an attack with all our forces in some other quarter.

When attack and defense in the very last stages of the game are so evenly balanced, and both our own men and those of our opponent are so favorably placed, that, unless the adversary voluntarily gives way, neither party can improve his position; when, in other words, the move ceases to be a privilege, "time" (the right to move, that is, to do something useful), will assume a new and very different character. In such positions as are very frequent in well contested games, and the occurrence of which can often with certainty be forecalculated, to have to move means often a *loss* in the working power of your pieces, and it may consequently lose you the game. We shall speak of this as the *principle of exhaustion* (that is, exhaustion of moves to *improve* your position). This principle will manifest itself in the great care with which the two combatants hold back certain moves, which either would improve their position, or at least not affect it harmfully, until a favorable opportunity has arrived for executing them.

The principle of exhaustion may be illustrated by the diagrams.

BLACK

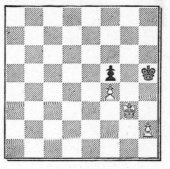

WHITE

White, maneuvering on the KR or KKt file, has no chance to force the win; there is not sufficient space at his disposal. For instance, after (1) K - R3, K - R3; (2) K - R4, K - Kt3, he would have to recede; therefore we must leave that quarter of the board to the Black King. Our KRP will consequently be a weakness, and it will be wise to hold it back as long as possible. The best position for the Black King to occupy will be Kt5. Whenever he will occupy that, our King must be ready to march to K3 or K5. From this we deduce the following line of play:

1. K - R3	K - R3
2. K - Kt2	K - R4
3. K - Kt3	K - R3

The first manifestation of the principle.

4. K - B2	K - R4
5. K - K2	

Not (5) K - K3, as (5) . . . K - Kt5 would win a Pawn.

5. . . .	K - R5
6. K - Q3	K - Kt5
7. K - K3	K - R6
8. K - Q4	K x P
9. K - K5 winning	

BLACK

WHITE

White has two chances of winning, the one based on his passed Pawn, the other on the weakness of the Black RP. The Black K occupies at present a position of advantage in regard to both. This is changed by the following maneuver:

1. K - Q5	K - B1

If (1) . . . K - Q1; (2) K - Q6, K - B1; (3) P - B7 and wins.

2. K - B4	K - Q1
3. K - Q4	K - B1
4. K - Q5	K - B2
5. K - B5	

Now the move is changed, and White wins easily; or,

4. . . .	K - Q1
5. K - Q6	K - B1
6. P - B7	K - Kt2
7. K - Q7	

and mates in a few more moves.

An ending by Locock:

BLACK

WHITE

White has two dangerous attacks; the one against the weak Black KKtP, the K threatening it from KB4; the object of the other is to advance his P - K5, supported by the K at Q4. Therefore, when the White King will be at K3, the Black K must be able to occupy in that moment KKt4; and when the White King will stand on Q4, the Black King must prevent the threatened advance by marching to KB3. If then the White King is at Q3, ready to go in one move to either of these squares, the hostile King must stand on Kt3. Thus, the different squares on each side correspond to each other. This mode of reasoning followed up, we shall come to the conclusion that White with the move draws, Black with the move loses.

For example, if Black moves first,

1. . . .	K - R1
2. K - Kt2	K - Kt1
3. K - Kt3	K - R2
4. K - B2	K - R3
5. K - Q2	K - R4
6. K - B3	K - Kt4
7. K - B4	K - Kt3
8. K - Q3	K - Kt4
9. K - K3 and wins; or	
8. . . .	K - B3
9. K - Q4	K - Kt3
10. P - K5	P x P ch
11. K x P	K - B2
12. K - B5 winning	

Now let White have the move.

1. K - B2	K - R2
2. K - Q2	K - R3
3. K - K2	K - R4
4. K - Q2	K - R3
5. K - B2	K - R2
6. K - B3	K - Kt2
7. K - B4	K - B2
8. K - Q4	K - B3
9. K - Q3	K - Kt3
10. K - K3	K - Kt4, etc.

Another difficult position:

BLACK

WHITE

This position depends also on the principle of exhaustion. Black's points of advantage, from where he attacks the White Pawn, are three—K7, K6, KB5. The most forward and, therefore, best of these is K7. Whenever the Black King is there, the White King must be ready to occupy KKt2; and whenever the Black King marches to K6, the White King must take the point KKt3. The game will run therefore—

1. K - R1	K - Q7
2. K - R2	K - Q6
3. K - R3	K - Q5
4. K - Kt4	K - K6
5. K - Kt3	K - K7
6. K - Kt2	K - Q8
7. K - R1 (or R3) and draws	

An attempt to force one of the passed Pawns will fail.

1. K - R1	P - Kt5
2. K - Kt2, and draws	

Black with the move will win.

1. . . .	K - K8
2. K - Kt2	K - K7
3. K - Kt3	K - B8
4. K - R3	K - B7
5. K - Kt4	K - Kt7 winning

The following positions are illustrative of the power of the passed Pawn:

BLACK

WHITE

White wins by a clever stroke, in which all the powers of the Pawn at Kt7 are made use of.

1. R - B8 ch !	R x R
2. Q x P ch	K x Q
3. P x R(Kt) ch and wins	

The above is more of a mid game combination than an end game type; but even backed by very little force, a passed Pawn can be very dangerous.

BLACK

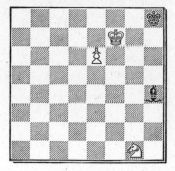

WHITE

1. Kt - B3	B - Q1
2. Kt - K5	K - R2
3. Kt - Kt4	K - R1
4. Kt - B6	

and wins, as Black has to move; if (3) . . ., B - R5 (Kt4); (4) Kt - B6 ch would obstruct the Bishop's line and therefore win.

BLACK

WHITE

1. B - Q4	B - Kt6
2. B - R7	B - B5
3. B - Kt8	B - K6
4. B - B7	B - R2
5. B - Kt6	

and wins in a few more moves. In both of the latter cases the King of the winning party is exceedingly well placed.

BLACK

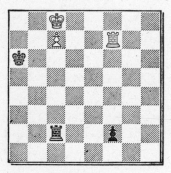

WHITE

The difference in the position of the Kings decides the struggle.

1. K - Kt8	R - Kt7 ch
2. K - R8	R - B7
3. R - B6 ch	K - R4

If . . . K - Kt4, (4) . . . K - Kt8 would speedily win.

4. K - Kt8	R - Kt7 ch
5. K - R7	R - B7
6. R - B5 ch	K - R5

7. K - Kt7	R - Kt7 ch
8. K - R6	R - B7
9. R - B4 ch	K - R6
10. K - Kt6	R - Kt7 ch
11. K - R5	R - B7
12. R - B3 ch	K - R7
13. R x P	

and wins by Queen against Rook.

White wins:

BLACK

WHITE

1. . . .	R - Kt7 ch
2. K - B1	R - Kt5
3. P - B8(R)	

If P Queens instead, . . . R - B5 ch, sacrificing itself, would force the stalemate.

3. . . .	R - QR5
4. R - QR8	K - Kt5

An excellent move. White threatened P - R6 - R7, and then a check with his Rook. If now (5) P - R6, K - B6, threatening mate, will force the draw, for instance, (6) K - K1, K - K6; (7) K - Q1, K - Q6; (8) K - B1, K - B6; (9) K - Kt1, R - Kt5 ch, and so on

5. K - K2	K - B4
6. P - R6	K - B3

not K - K3, as (7) P - R7, K - Q2; (8) R - KR8 would gain the Rook.

7. K - Q3

The decisive maneuver. The King comes now to the support of the Pawn, in order to liberate the Rook, while Black can do nothing to change the position to his advantage. The square QR7 is left free for the King, to allow him a place of safety against the checks of the Black Rook.

7. . . .	K - Kt2
8. K - B3	K - R2
9. K - Kt3	R - R4
10. K - Kt4	R - R8
11. K - Kt5	R - Kt8 ch
12. K - B6	R - B8 ch
13. K - Kt7	R - Kt8 ch
14. K - R7	

Without this place of refuge the game would never be won. Now it is a very simple matter.

14. . . .	K - Kt2
15. R - Kt8	R - QR8
16. R - Kt6	K - B2
17. K - Kt7 winning easily.	

BLACK

WHITE

Here White wins by his superior K position and because his Pawns are further advanced than those of Black.

1. K - B4

It is necessary to time the winning maneuver correctly. Therefore we must not at once march to K4.

1. . . .	K - B1
2. K - K4	P - B4
3. K - Q3	K - K1
4. P - K7	

The right moment for the advance. Now all Black's movements are forced.

4. . . .	K - Q2
5. K - B4	K - K1
6. K x P	P - Q6
7. K - Q6	P - Q7
8. K - K6	P - Q8(Q)
9. P - B7 mate	

BLACK

WHITE

1. P - R5   B - R3

The White QRP has only to pass one more black square, and that within two moves; therefore the Bishop must hurry to stop it.

2. P - Kt5 ch !   B x P

Now the Bishop is obstructed by his own King (if (2) . . . K x P; (3) P - R6 wins).

3. K - K4   B - R5
4. K - B3

and the Pawn will Queen.

When the end game stage is nearing, the power of the various pieces is altered to a marked degree. Different issues being at stake, different measures must be adopted, and ideas, correct in the early part of the game, become sensibly modified. The value of each piece varies, of course, with each end game position in a greater or lesser degree; but the men have a certain average value, which will serve as guide. This value will be determined—

(*a*) By their fighting capacity against the adverse King as an aggressive piece,

(*b*) and against passed Pawns,

(*c*) and finally their *reach* or power of offense, when obstructions (as is usual in end games) are few.

Let us first consider the King. Being placed in opposition to the adverse King, he will take three squares from him, and can thus hinder him from advancing. He can, single-handed, stop three united passed Pawns, not advanced beyond the sixth row; and two, one of which is on the seventh row. He can attack every square on the board, and that, if he is in a central point, for instance, at K4, in no more than three moves.

His reach is totally uninfluenced by obstructions other than the natural limits of the board. He is, therefore, a powerful weapon, if well developed in one of the central points or near important points; he can, however, never be used as an instrument of obstruction, never be exposed to any direct attack, which sensibly diminishes his offensive value against strong pieces of offense.

Black: MORPHY

White: HARRWITZ

The annexed position occurred in one of Morphy's match games. The game went on:

1. . . .	P - QR3 !
2. P - R4	P x P
3. RP x P	R - R1

The first advantage, an unopposed open file for the Rook, is now established.

4. Kt - Q2	R - R6
5. P - K4	P x P
6. Kt x P	Kt x Kt
7. B x Kt	R - QB6
8. B - B3	

Threatening now, of course, R - K8 ch - QKt8

8. . . .	K - B2
9. R - K4	B - B1
10. B - K2	B - B4
11. R - Q4	P - R4

Through this last move the important point at KB4 becomes strong.

12. K - B2	K - B3
13. R - Q2	B - B7
14. K - K1	B - K5
15. K - B2	K - B4

The White King is kept back by the Black Rook; the Black King, however, can advance unchecked.

16. R - R2	P - R5

forcing the way for his King, which will soon become a dangerous assailant.

17. P x P	K x P
18. R - R7	R - KR6
19. R x P	R - R7 ch
20. K - K1	K - K6

Crushing all resistance.

Black: STEINITZ

White: LASKER

In one of my match games with Mr. Steinitz the above position occurred, White to move.

1. KR - Q1	P - K4

If K - Q2 at once, P - KB4 will give White a good game.

2. B - K3	K - Q2
3. B - B5	R - R8
4. KR - Q2	K - K3
5. B - R3	P - Kt4
6. R - Q5	R - Kt3
7. K - Kt4	

Now the King actively enters into the fight.

7. . . .	P - Kt5

The initiation of a subtle counterattack which nearly succeeded in turning the tables.

8. K - R5   . . .

It might have been wiser first to accept the offered Pawn, thus: (8) P x P, R - K8; (9) K - R5, B - Q1; (10) R x P, R - R3 ch; (11) K - Kt4, R x P ch; (12) K - Kt3 remaining a Pawn ahead.

8. . . .	R - R3 ch
9. K x P	P - R4

Or (9) . . ., R - R8; (10) P x P, R - K8; (11) P - R3, R x P; (12) P - B4.

10. R - Q1	R x R
11. R x R	P x P
12. P x P	R - R1
13. K - Kt6	R - KKt1
14. K x P	R - Kt7
15. P - R4	R - R7
16. K - B6	

This maneuver makes the Black game untenable.

16. . . .	B x P
17. R x P ch	K - B2
18. K - Q5	B - B3

If (18) . . ., R - Q7 ch; (19) K x P, B - Kt6 ch; (20) P - B4, R x R; (21) B x R, P - R5; (22) B - B5, P - R6; (23) B - Kt1 and the four passed Pawns win easily against the Bishop.

19. R - Q7 ch	K - Kt3
20. K - K6	

To check the advance of the Black King.

If now (20) . . ., K - Kt4; (21) R - KB7, B - Q1; (22)

R - B8, B - Kt3; (23) B - K7 ch, K - Kt3; (24) R - Kt8 ch, K - R2; (25) K - B7 followed by B - B6 would draw the Black King into a mating net.

20. . . .	P - R5
21. R - Q1	P - R6
22. R - Kt1 ch	R - Kt7
23. R x R ch	P x R
24. B - B5	

And wins after a few more moves with his passed Pawns.

Black: SALMON

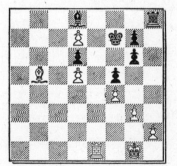

White: MORPHY

Another of Morphy's energetic end game attacks.

1. R - K8	R - B1
2. K - B2	P - Kt4
3. K - K3	P - Kt5
4. K - Q3	P - Kt4
5. B - B6	P x P
6. P x P	R - Kt1
7. K - B4	

The Black forces being all engaged by the combined action of the White Rook, passed Pawn and Bishop, the co-operation of the King is all that is necessary to decide the day.

7. . . .	R - B1
8. K - Kt5	R - Kt1
9. K - R6	R - B1
10. K - Kt7	R - Kt1
11. K - B8	B - Kt3
12. R x R	K x R
13. P - Q8(Q) ch	B x Q
14. K x B	Resigns

Examples concerning the power of the King could be readily multiplied. But we leave this for a future occasion, the King as an assailant, or as strong protective power being an essential element, indeed almost an organic part of each approximately even end game.

13. *The End Game* (CONCLUDED)

ANOTHER piece whose power increases the more the end game stage is approaching is the Rook. Its fighting capacity against the adverse King is enormous, and exactly what makes it a valuable instrument for attack as well as defense. In conjunction with its own King it can checkmate the hostile K driven to the edge of the board, and in combination with a Kt and P and a single obstruction it can give checkmate to the K on any square of the board (example, Rook at KB8, Kt at KKt6, P at KB5; opponent's King at KB7, one of his Pawns at KKt7).

Without any kind of support it can give untold checks to the adverse King, until the same is obliged to approach the Rook, perhaps against the best interests of his game, or forced to protect himself behind some kind of obstruction. On account of its attacking qualities, it is always a valuable ally when you want to force any obstructions out of the way, for instance, of passed Pawns; but it is less fit for fighting against them, and really too valuable a piece to be given away for such a purpose, if other alternatives are open. The best way to stop an adverse passed Pawn with a Rook is to place the Rook behind it, as its reach will increase the more the Pawn advances. It can stop and even win (if they are unsupported) two passed Pawns, of which one is on the sixth, the other on the fifth, row; but two passed Pawns on the sixth row will Queen against it if united. Used against advanced Pawns it is, therefore, not as manageable as the King, or even the Bishop, but it is the more dangerous to the Pawns before they assume a threatening attitude, as its reach is very great, and exactly calculated to serve against Pawns in their strongest position—that is, when they are abreast. It can attack, if unobstructed, any square of the board in one move, and will command thirteen at a time. This enables it to restrict the opposite King to a portion of the board.

The Bishop is very much less fit for assault against the King, or for restricting his approach, than the Rook. The Bishop can take away two squares from the King, and eventually give check and command two squares of the reach of the King. Its capacity for yielding support to passed Pawns is not very great, as the line in which the Pawn advances will usually contain some points where obstructions are totally safe against the Bishop. Its great value consists in two things: (1) That it can stop adverse Pawns from a long distance and from a number of squares. (2) That a Pawn and a Bishop may protect each other, so as to make both of them comparatively safe against the King or superior pieces. Its chess-board, however, contains only thirty-two squares, and whichever influence they may have on the issue of the game, very much determines its share in it; so that its importance may be exaggerated when you have the superiority of position, or almost annihilated when the opposite is the case.

The Knight is, unless circumstances are very favorable, the weakest piece of all. It may take two squares from the King, give check, and besides take away one square from him: but the adverse King may approach it then, and get rid of it if no support is near. Its great power is that he cannot be obstructed. When obstructions abound, and when it can occupy a strong point near the enemy's line, it can be an invaluable ally. Its reach never exceeds eight points, situated in a circle, and it may be obliged to take five moves to cross the board from one point to another (for instance, the two diagonally opposite corner points). On an extended field of battle it must, therefore, choose the wing to which he will give his support, or very much lose in value.

To refer to the oft mooted question, "Which piece is stronger, the Bishop or the Knight?" it is clear that the value of the Bishop undergoes greater changes than that of the Knight. If experience has shown that, on an average, during the opening or middle game, the Bishop will be at least as strong as the Knight, this will be the more true the more obstructions disappear, that is, in endings with only a few Pawns scattered about the board. In complicated end game positions, where Pawns partly form blocks, the Knight will find its best chance. The value of two Bishops varies, of course, as they dominate the whole chess-board, very much less than that of one; in consequence, two Bishops are, as a rule, appreciably stronger than two Knights or a Bishop and a Knight.

From a correspondence game:

BLACK

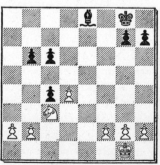

WHITE

1. Kt - K4		P - QKt4
2. P - QR3		

Now all the black squares on the Q side are in possession of White; nor can this be changed, as the Black King is needed on the K side to fight against the White Pawns.

2. . . .	B - Kt3
3. P - B3	K - B2
4. K - B2	K - K3
5. K - K3	P - R3
6. P - KKt4	K - Q4
7. Kt - B3 ch	K - Q3
8. P - B4	B - K1

It would have been more advisable to keep the Bishop in the rear of the advancing Pawns.

As a rule, pieces function most effectively against passed Pawns when placed *behind* the Pawns.

9. P - B5	B - Q2
10. Kt - K4 ch	K - K2

If (10) . . ., K - Q4; (11) P - B6 will force the exchange of Kt v. B. and the extra Pawn will easily win.

11. K - B4	B - K1
12. K - K5	B - B2
13. P - KR4	B - Q4
14. P - Kt5	P x P
15. P x P	B - Kt1
16. P - Kt6	Resigns

as P - B6 will soon prove decisive.

Another correspondence game; Black moves:

BLACK

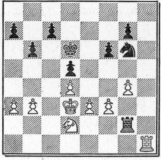

WHITE

1. . . .	P - QB4

Strong, and embarrassing to White. The Pawn engages the QP, which is the only White piece that commands the point K5. It can, therefore, not take the hostile Pawn, as after (2) P x P ch, P x P, White has no means to stop the check at K4, which would soon prove fatal to him.

2. R - R7

Unsatisfactory enough; but the Kt cannot move to any square improving his position, and without exposing the White Pawns to the attack of the Rook.

2. . . .	P x P
3. P x P	Kt - B5 ch
4. K - B3	Kt - K3

Now White can do nothing effectual. If the Rook moves, Black will win the QP.

5. K - Q3	P - R4
6. K - K3	R - Kt8

This maneuver with the Rook is splendid. He threatens now R - QB8 - B6 ch winning the QP. White cannot frustrate that plan, *e. g.*, (7) K - Q3, R - QB8; (8) P - R4, Kt - B5 ch; (9) K - K3, P - KKt4; (10) K - B2, R - Q8, etc.

7. R - R8	R - QB8
8. R - QKt8	R - B6 ch
9. K - B2	Kt x P
10. R x P ch	K - K4
11. R - Kt7	K - B5

If now (12) R x P, R - B7; (13) K - K1, K - K6; (14) R - K7 ch, K - Q6; (15) Kt - B1, Kt x P ch; (16) K - Q1, P - Q5; and White has no satisfactory move left.

12. P - Kt5	R - K6

and White resigns, for if (13) P x P, P x P; (14) R - KB7, R - K7 ch.

The following position occurred in a match game at Hastings, 1895, between Messrs. Schlechter and Tchigorin.

Black: TCHIGORIN

White: SCHLECHTER

It was White's turn to move, and the game went on:

1. P - QKt4

A Pawn move without a clearly defined purpose is to be criticized. The P at Kt4 takes away a good square from the Kt, which that piece ought to have occupied at once in order to threaten Kt - Q5, and to force the advance P - B3, which would greatly increase the strength of the B. Moreover, it leaves a strong point at QB5 to the Black Kts, which White can only guard by another advance of a Pawn.

1. . . .	R(Q) - KKt1
2. R - KKt1	

He ought not to leave the important Q file with his Rook. All defensive purposes could be served just as well by (2) P - R3, which would enable him to reply to (2) . . ., P - Kt5 with (3) BP x P, P x P, (4) P - R4 and to (2) . . ., P - R5 with P - Kt4.

2. . . .	P - Kt5
3. P - KB4	Kt - Q1
4. P - B5	Kt - B2
5. Kt - B2	Kt - Q3
6. B - B5	Kt - Kt3

Not (6) . . ., Kt x B, as (7) P x Kt, Kt moves; (8) P - B6 would follow.

7. Kt - Q1

Now, decidedly, R - Q1 was the indicated move, when, for instance, (7) . . ., R - Q1; (8) R x Kt, R x R; (9) R - Q1 would lead to a probable draw.

7. . . .	Kt(Kt3) - B1
8. Kt - K3	K - B2

Now the KP has become indefensible.

9. Kt - Q5	P - B3
10. Kt - B7	Kt x KP
11. QR - Q1	Kt x B
12. P x Kt	R - Q1
13. Kt - K6	R x R
14. R x R	K - K2

Black: TCHIGORIN

White: SCHLECHTER

15. P - R4

In thus opening up files for the Black Rook he plays Black's game, (15) P - B4 is by far preferable. Neither the Black Kt nor the R will then ever be able to obtain good positions. (15) . . ., P - R5 could then, for instance, be answered by (16) P x P; R x P; (17) R - Q8, Kt - R2; (18) R - QR8 winning the piece.

15. . . .	P x P e.p.
16. R - KR1	K - B2
17. R x P	Kt - K2
18. P - KKt4	P - R5
19. P - B4	Kt - Kt3

A pretty little move which threatens Kt - B1.

20. P x Kt ch	K x Kt
21. P - Kt7	R - KKt1
22. R x P	R x P
23. K - K3	K - B2

It remains to force the exchange of the last P on the K side, in order to have there all lines free, and a clear superiority.

24. P - Kt4	K - Kt3

If the plausible (24) . . ., K - Kt1 instead, then (25) K - K4, R - R2; (26) R x R, K x R; (27) K - B5, K - Kt2; (28) P - KKt5, P x P; (29) K x KtP, drawing without difficulty.

25. R - R8	P - B4
26. P x P ch	K x P
27. R - R5 ch	. . .

(27) R - B8 ch would find its reply in K - K3; (28) R - K8 ch, K - Q2; (29) R x P, R - Kt6 ch; (30) K moves R - Kt6, when Black will remain with a winning advantage.

27. . . .	K - K3
28. R - R6 ch	K - Q2
29. P - Kt5	RP x P
30. P x P	P x P
31. K - K4	R - K2
32. R - QKt6	K - B2
33. R x P	K - B3
34. R - R5	R - K1

This maneuver with the Rook, which wins a move, decides the game. The White King dare not move, as

otherwise the Black KP advances still further; so all
White's moves are forced.

35.	R - R7	R - K3
36.	R - R5	R - K2
37.	R - R1	K x P
38.	R - B1 ch	K - Q3
39.	R - Q1 ch	K - B3
40.	R - B1 ch	K - Q2
41.	R - B5	K - Q3
42.	R - B2	P - Kt4
43.	R - QKt2	K - B4

And White resigned the struggle which Black had mas-
terfully conducted.